DATE DUE

~~June 5~~		
MR 25 '02		
5/2/09		

DEMCO 38-296

CONSCIOUSNESS UNFOLDING

Other Writings of Joel S. Goldsmith

Consciousness
Unfolding

Joel S. Goldsmith

Edited By
Lorraine Sinkler

I-Level

Acropolis Books, Publisher
Lakewood, CO

Riverside Community College
Library
4800 Magnolia Avenue
Riverside, CA 92506

BF 639 .G558 1999

Goldsmith, Joel S., 1892-
1964.

Consciousness unfolding

_UNFOLDING
Edition 1999
© 1962, 1990 by Joel Goldsmith

All Bible quotations are taken from THE KING JAMES VERSION

Published by Acropolis Books, Publisher, under its *I*-Level imprint, under an arrangement with Citadel Press, an imprint of Carol Publishing Group.
All rights reserved.

Printed in the United States of America.

No part of this book may be used or reproduced in any manner whatsoever without written permission except in the case of brief quotations embodied in critical articles and reviews.

For information contact:

Acropolis Books, Inc.
Lakewood, Colorado

http://www.acropolisbooks.com

Library of Congress Cataloging-in-Publication Data

Goldsmith, Joel S., 1892–1964.
    Consciousness unfolding / Joel S. Goldsmith; edited by Lorraine Sinkler.
    - - 1ˢᵗ Acropolis books ed.
        p.   cm.
    Originally published: Secaucus, N. J. : University Books, 1974, ©1962.
    Includes bibliographical references.
    ISBN 1-889051-40-3 (hardcover : alk. paper)
    ISBN 1-889051-39-X (paperback : alk. paper)
    1. New Thought.   I. Sinkler, Lorraine.   II. Title.
BF639.G558   1999
299'.93–dc21   99-10863
                                                                              CIP

This book is printed on acid free paper that meets the American National Standards Institute Z 39.48 Standard

Riverside Community College
Library
4800 Magnolia Avenue
Riverside, CA 92506

Except the Lord build the house,
they labour in vain that build it. . . .

—Psalm 127

"Illumination dissolves all material ties and binds men together with the golden chains of spiritual understanding; it acknowledges only the leadership of the Christ; it has no ritual or rule but the divine, impersonal universal Love; no other worship than the inner Flame that is ever lit at the shrine of Spirit. This union is the free state of spiritual brotherhood. The only restraint is the discipline of Soul; therefore, we know liberty without license; we are a united universe without physical limits, a divine service to God without ceremony or creed. The illumined walk without fear—by Grace."

—*The Infinite Way* by Joel S. Goldsmith

TABLE OF CONTENTS

TABLE OF CONTENTS

TABLE OF CONTENTS

Consciousness
Unfolding

~ 1 ~

GOD IS INDIVIDUAL CONSCIOUSNESS

To experience God unfolding as individual consciousness is the purpose of the Infinite Way. It is a revelation *within* your own being *of* your own being, an experience which takes place within you.

The kingdom of God is within you. As a matter of fact, you are the individualization of all that God is: "Son, all that I have is thine."[1] Therefore, the work of the Infinite Way is to reveal the Infinite Invisible within you to that part of you which we call the outer, the visible, or human being, which, in reality, is not a human being at all, but a divine being. The world interprets the human scene in human terms, and therefore that which is appearing in and to the world as a human being, that is, as you or as me, through this work, will receive from within the depth of his own being the revelation of his true nature.

The impartation, then, in this work, is not from one intellect to another. It is divine Consciousness revealing Itself as individual being. The things of God are foolishness with men, but "if any man have ears to hear, let him hear."[2] Let this message solidify as your own individual consciousness; let the words go round and round in your own consciousness until you catch the inner vision of what is written in these pages: Then, it will become your own. After that, you will be able to teach it, but not in my words, in my language, or by using my experiences; it will become your own individual unfoldment of this same truth. In metaphysics, you cannot teach the letter of truth and get very far. The real teaching is the impartation of spiritual consciousness. If I give you something that I have merely heard or read or memorized, it will bring forth no real response from within you. Unless the teaching has become my very consciousness, you will not be able to take it in. The only truth which you will receive in consciousness from reading this book is that which is a living part of my own being. You will catch the fire of such truth, and it will take root in you.

Unfortunately, in metaphysical practice, too many statements are made to patients which have not been demonstrated and which have not become part of the consciousness of the practitioner or teacher. There is no more profound truth in the world than the statement: "There is no error." In the voicing of that statement, the whole mortal universe should collapse, but no matter how many times that statement has been or is voiced, the world goes right on in the same old way. Why? Because the statement, "There is no error," has not become an idea embodied in consciousness.

A practitioner may say to a patient: "There is only one life, and that life is God. This, that is appearing to you, is a suggestion, is not reality, and is no part of your being." When the practitioner has the conviction and consciousness of that truth, very often the error disappears—the disease, sin, or lack disappears. But, if the practitioner is merely repeating what he has heard, what he has read in books, or something he remembers, and is only hoping or wishing it were true, then, it will have no power.

The things of God are foolishness with men, but so, also, are the things of men foolishness with God. Try to remember that, when you are tempted to take any of your human problems to God. To think in terms of a sick body being made well by God, or of unemployment being solved by God, or of a war being stopped by God, or of your favorite candidate being elected by God is foolishness. The things of men, the things of this Adam-dream—this whole world existence—are unknown to God. That is what makes healing possible. Disease has no real existence; it is unknown to God. Inevitably, when disease and distress hit up against a consciousness that knows this truth, they fall because of their own nothingness.

Always remember that, in the spiritual world, teaching and being taught are activities. Go within your own consciousness and pray to God. Pray that your teacher and teaching will be revealed to you. Pray: "Father, lead me to the one; lead me to the teacher; lead me to my teacher."

The import and purpose of the teaching of the Infinite Way is to unfold your Soul, to develop the Soul capacities of your own being. You must select a teacher of spiritual truth with much more care than you would select any other kind of a teacher. There is nothing more sacred than spiritual teaching. There is nothing that will do more to lift you out of a mortal, material sense of life than correct spiritual teaching.

For the spiritual teachers, teaching is a sacred ministry. A teacher must so live in the consciousness of God as to be able to impart divine realities. That can be done only from a state of consciousness which is acting and living this truth. From the student's point of view, spiritual teaching is also a sacred ministry because it means the development of his own Soul. It means lifting him out of the dangers, diseases, and limitations of mortal existence. Therefore, be led of the Spirit. Make this search for your spiritual teacher a sacred rite. Then, when you have received some instruction, or have found a book, sit still with it for a while; abide in it; give it an opportunity to work within you.

Spiritual Consciousness

The subject matter of this book is the unfolding of consciousness. That means God revealing, God disclosing Itself to you—infinite, indivisible Consciousness revealing, unfolding, and disclosing Itself as individual consciousness. Therefore, this work is an individual matter, and it must be attained through individual effort—through *your* effort. Success will come about in proportion as you attain some measure of spiritual consciousness.

Spiritual consciousness is that state of consciousness from which world beliefs have disappeared in some measure. Spiritual consciousness, or Christ consciousness, is that state of consciousness which no longer reacts to things in the outer realm. You are infinite, spiritual consciousness. You are the law unto your own experience. Nothing external—nothing existing as effect—can have power or jurisdiction over you. You are the law unto every effect. Therefore, when you love, hate, or fear something in the external, you are hypnotized into a state of mortal consciousness.

In the human picture, the most sought after thing that there is on earth is money—first money, then sex. These are the things that the world, as a human world, seeks so zealously. Mortal consciousness puts value in the dollar bill and says, "This will do much for me!" But spiritual consciousness puts no faith in it. It knows the true nature of supply: "Supply is my individual consciousness. It is God consciousness individualized as me. Regardless of what my need may seem to be, whether it is a dollar bill or a yacht, it must unfold from the infinity of my own consciousness. Therefore, I take no thought either for a dollar bill or for a yacht."

This is the attitude you must learn to take, and it is the attitude you must practice until it becomes a reality. Humanly, this attitude is not natural to the adult. On the contrary, to a child it is entirely natural. A child will throw a twenty-dollar gold piece out of the window, because he has not yet learned to put a value on such things. His sense of value is love, the love he has for his mother and father, and the love they have for him. That is his supply, and he knows it. As long as there is that love between child and parent, the daily food, the clothing and the home are forthcoming as a matter of course. Therefore, *love* is the child's sense of supply. Only as he grows out of this sense of love, will his sense of supply change and become fifty cents, or a million dollars.

We must return to that same childlike trust we had in our childhood days. The Master told us that we must become "as a little child."[3] Let us go back to that point where we no longer rely on the dollar bill for our supply, but begin to understand that Love, Consciousness, or spirituality is our supply, and that as long as we have the presence of Love, we shall have all things added unto us. That is one step in the unfoldment and revelation of God—divine Consciousness appearing as love and meeting our so-called human needs. You can easily understand that for a while, every time you handle money, you will consciously need to remember that it is not supply, but that it is the effect of Love; it is the effect of the presence of God appearing as your consciousness. In this way you will gradually develop within yourself an attitude which recognizes that the dollar bill is not the reality of your supply.

An example of this is the case of the Hindu couple who took up the spiritual life, and with their begging bowls set out upon the way. One day, while walking along the road, the husband in front and the wife just behind him, the man bent over, picked something up from the dirt, rubbed it on his robe, and put the object in his pocket. The wife quickly asked him what he had found. When he showed her a diamond, her rebuke was swift and sharp, "We are living the spiritual life. In what way is the diamond of greater value than the dirt which you rubbed off the diamond?" No, the value is not in the diamond. The value is in our consciousness, which is the substance, the form, the principle, and the law unto the diamond. As long as *I* * exist—and *I* is God—*I* will be the law manufacturing, in whatever form is necessary, that which is my need.

All Power Is in Consciousness

Let us suppose that someone calls and says, "I am sick. Give me some help." Now, heretofore, when someone has said, "I do not feel well," you have probably immediately denied it, but we are going to learn not

---

* The word "I," italicized, refers to God.

to deny it. We are not going to put up a "wall" against illness. Instead, our response will be: "What about it? Is it power? Is it a presence? Is it reality? Or is all power the consciousness of the individual, which is the law of health? And this growth, this pain, or this lack, is it a law? No, of course, it is not."

Right from the beginning, that is our realization with every claim, with every call that is made upon us for help. We may find ourselves saying, "So what?" or anything else that will help us to agree with our adversary. The healing principle is: "Agree with thine adversary."[4] You cannot fight anything with which you agree. The moment you fight, wrestle, or battle any claim that comes to you, you are setting up an adversary rather than coming into agreement or at-one-ment with what appears to be error, but which, in reality, is only an illusion—if there can be reality to an illusion. The moment that you fight or battle error in any form, you have set it up as something which must be removed, and there is no telling how long the healing will take. The only instantaneous healings are the ones that take place when the consciousness of the practitioner knows, when the practitioner is convinced, that there is no power or presence to that thing claiming to be an erroneous manifestation.

Is there such a thing as healing possible while you are believing in or attempting to heal the condition? No, healing comes in the recognition that the consciousness of the individual is God, or that God is the consciousness of the individual. Thus, the consciousness of the individual is the law unto every condition. In biblical language, "greater is he that is in you, than he that is in the world."[5]

Consciousness, God—the consciousness of the individual, is always the law; it is always the presence; it is always the reality. If something does appear externally, it still is only an effect and, as effect, it cannot be law. As effect, it cannot be cause. As effect, it cannot be power. No effect in the world has power over another effect: That is a spiritual law. Consciousness is all power. All power comes from on High. God gave man dominion. In other words, God, universal Consciousness, gave to man, to individualized spiritual consciousness, all power over everything that exists in the realm of effect, whether a tiny flower or a planet in the sky.

The moment you acknowledge something in the realm of effect as having dominion over you, you have made that a law for yourself, and you suffer from it until you reverse your stand and realize that it is impossible that I, the fullness of God made manifest, the infinite Son of God, I of whom God said, "All that I have is thine,"[6] should be at the mercy of anything in the outer realm, of anyone, of any condition or any set of conditions.

As you realize that God, infinite, divine Consciousness, is the consciousness of the individual, and is the law unto the universe, you take possession of your life, and have some degree of mastery over it. Otherwise, you are the victim of some particular form of government, of a certain amount of dollars, or of germs, infection, or contagion. Only in the degree that you can realize your oneness with God, only in the degree that you can realize that you are the very presence of God, acting as a law unto your universe, only in that degree, can you achieve mastery over your existence!

Where God is, I am, "*I and my Father are one . . .*[7] *the place whereon [I stand] is holy ground . . .*[8] *If I make my bed in hell,*"[9] I, *God, am there. And that* I am *is a law unto* *everything appearing as the external universe, or as the universe of effect.**

To give up our fear of anything in the world of effect, is the first step in attaining Christ consciousness. Christ consciousness has no fear of a disease or of a sin, and It has no dread of it. It just says: "Neither do I condemn thee: go and sin no more[10] . . . Who did hinder you[11] . . . Take up thy bed and walk."[12] And why? Because in this way we agree with the adversary and acknowledge that the only power is the consciousness of the individual. Every time you see sin, lack or limitation in the external scene, instead of jumping in to give a treatment, say: "No, you are not fooling me! You exist as an effect of some kind or other, but you are only the railroad tracks coming together, and if I could see you as you are, the tracks would be in their right places. My eyes are not fooling me any more."

Do not give treatments! Do not give treatments to God and His universe! And remember that there is no other! Treatments, in themselves, are of no value. Nobody in the whole history of metaphysics has ever changed one condition of reality by means of treatment. Not one single improvement has ever been made in the entire spiritual realm through treatment. Treatments are

---

* The italicized portions of this book are spontaneous meditations which have come to the author during periods of uplifted consciousness and are not in any sense intended to be used as affirmations, denials, or formulas. They have been inserted in this book from time to time to serve as examples of the free flowing of the Spirit. As the reader practices the presence, he, too, in his exalted moments, will receive ever new and fresh inspiration as the outpouring of the Spirit.

of no value, but prayer is. Pray without ceasing because prayer is the unfoldment of your own consciousness. Prayer is God disclosing Itself to you. Prayer is God revealing Its truth to your individual awareness.

Prayer is the disclosing of the divine reality to our individual consciousness. Turning within, watching, always listening for the divine reality, is the secret of spiritual living. And that is the secret that ultimately discloses God to us as our individual being and as our individual selfhood. In this withinness, and in this only, are found harmony, peace, joy, power, and dominion.

The spiritual universe must now unfold itself to you. You must not be concerned with or disturbed about what is going on in the human world. By this I do not mean that you should hide your head in the sand. You still go about your affairs, doing things according to your highest sense of right. But you will have no concern about the results of your efforts when you have lived up to that sense.

Remember this: There is an unseen, invisible universe. That is what you are seeking. "Flesh and blood cannot inherit the kingdom of God."[13] It does not say "diseased flesh and diseased blood"; it just says "flesh and blood." Nothing that exists as form can inherit the kingdom of God. Nothing that exists to your mortal sense can ever be brought into the kingdom of God. We are dedicated, now, not to trying to improve human conditions, but to the revelation of God and the spiritual universe, unfolding as our individual consciousness. There is an infinite, invisible universe. There is a world of spiritual ideas, but this world has no relationship to the world that we can see, hear, touch, taste, or smell. What we are aware of in the world of the senses is the distorted view of the divine idea, of the real universe, which we are seeing "through a glass, darkly."[14] Right where we appear to be, God is. Right where every bit of mortal phenomena seems to be, the spiritual universe is. We are but beholding it "through a glass, darkly," calling it mortal and material. In its real essence, it is spiritual and divine.

Consciousness Appears as Loaves and Fishes

After these things Jesus went over the sea of Galilee, which is the sea of Tiberias.

And a great multitude followed him, because they saw his miracles which he did on them that were diseased.

And Jesus went up into a mountain, and there he sat with his disciples.

And the Passover, a feast of the Jews, was nigh.

When Jesus then lifted his eyes, and saw a great company come unto him, he saith unto Philip, Whence shall we buy bread, that these may eat?

And this he said to prove him: for he himself knew what he would do.

Philip answered him, Two hundred pennyworth of bread is not sufficient for them, that every one of them may take a little.

One of his disciples, Andrew, Simon Peter's brother, saith unto him,

There is a lad here, which hath five barley loaves and two small fishes: but what are they among so many?

And Jesus said, Make the men sit down.[15]

The appearance was lack and material limitation. The first response of most of us in such a situation is, "I have only fifty cents, and I need five dollars." It is at this point that material sense begins to worry itself into what the world calls ulcers. In our teaching, we do as the Master did. Instantly, we turn away from the picture. Will fifty cents, or five dollars, really meet our need? Is that what is necessary for us to have in order to meet the need? Or is it the presence of a divine Consciousness appearing as individual consciousness? Is it not that which will meet our need, and nothing else?

If you will remember this lesson, you will never again look to loaves and fishes, or to coins and bills, or judge by finite sense and finite numbers the depth and boundlessness of God's universe. We have found, not how to take a few loaves and fishes and multiply them; we have found the law of love.

Finite sense will begin with a hundred dollars and say: "When I have a million dollars—"But no matter how much you multiply loaves and fishes—or dollars—you never will be satisfied. Satisfaction comes only when you can look at what you have in the external realm and say: "That is not my need. My need is the recognition that within me is the kingdom of God, that within my consciousness is the spiritual universe, and that from out of the depth of my consciousness flows the infinity of my being." It has nothing to do with loaves and fishes.

To arrive at this state of consciousness takes practice because again and again, we shall be tempted to look at the loaves and fishes and say, "I have or you have"; or "I have not; I want." Then is when we must remember not to be tempted, but to turn away from numbers and amounts and degrees, and realize: "Nothing out there will meet my need. No amount of things will meet my need. My need can only be met by the realization of the infinity of my own consciousness." And then we shall be dying daily to mortal, material sense, and we shall be reborn of the Spirit. In other words, Spirit will become the tangible substance of our universe to us; Consciousness will become the tangible substance—the form and the amount of everything in the external realm. And because Consciousness is infinite, its appearance will be infinitely manifest.

Infinite Consciousness cannot appear as only one idea, or as two ideas, or even as a thousand. It must appear as all the ideas you will ever need throughout eternity. It cannot appear as one number, or two. It must appear as all the numbers you will ever have need of from now throughout eternity. We are not using spiritual truth to multiply a few pieces of matter. We are turning away from the belief that there is presence and power in the external, and turning to our understanding that infinite Consciousness is appearing as our individual consciousness.

Acknowledging the Source

And Jesus said, Make the men sit down. Now there was much grass in the place. So the men sat down, in number about five thousand.

And Jesus took the loaves; and when he had given thanks, he distributed to the disciples, and the disciples to them that were set down; and likewise of the fishes as much as they would.[16]

Why did he give thanks? Why was that a part of the ritual? You know he was not under orders to give thanks to anybody, so in giving thanks he must have been putting the principle into operation.

Giving thanks is an acknowledgment of the Source. Giving thanks is an acknowledgment of the Cause. So when we say, "Thank you, Father, I am," we are showing forth our conviction that our supply does not come from any human being, but that it comes from the

Father. It comes, not from our own human cleverness, ingenuity, or personality. It comes forth from the Father. So, giving thanks is a recognition of the Source: Consciousness. Without the recognition that Consciousness is the source, there is no further demonstration. When we recognize God, the infinite Consciousness of our being, as the source of all that comes to us, then our "Thank you, Father," is our acknowledgment of the nothingness of human selfhood and human effort. It is a recognition of the presence and power of God as the source of all that comes to us as the fulfilment of every need.

In every avenue of your experience, gratitude plays a much greater part than you perhaps realize. Gratitude is not something that concerns the other person. It is your relationship, your contact, with God. It is your own individual at-one-ment with God. Actually, you never need to say, "Thank you," outwardly to another person who has been an avenue or channel for good for you. Of course, we do, as a form of courtesy, but unless that outer expression of gratitude is accompanied by the inner realization that God, our consciousness, is the source of that for which we are grateful, we are being grateful to the wrong source, and we have lost the essence of the true sense of gratitude. The "Thank you, Father," of Jesus was his silent recognition that God is the cause and the effect of any and every amount of loaves and fishes.

When they were filled, he said unto his disciples, Gather up the fragments that remain, that nothing be lost.

Therefore they gathered *them* together, and filled twelve baskets with the fragments of the five barley loaves, which remained over and above unto them that had eaten.

Then those men, when they had seen the miracle that Jesus did, said, This is of a truth that prophet that should come into the world.

When Jesus therefore perceived that they would come and take him by force, to make him a king, he departed again into a mountain himself alone.

And when even was *now* come, his disciples went down unto the sea,

And entered into a ship, and went over the sea toward Capernaum. And it was now dark, and Jesus was not come to them.

And the sea arose by reason of a great wind that blew.

So when they had rowed about five and twenty or thirty furlongs, they see Jesus walking on the sea, and drawing nigh unto the ship: and they were afraid.

But he saith unto them, It is I; be not afraid.[17]

What were they afraid of? Of something external, of something in the form of an effect—in other words, of a storm, of wind and waves. And what was his answer to that storm, and what is the answer to every storm? "Be not afraid; it is I." The *I* is God, divine Consciousness, appearing as individual consciousness. Therefore, to every "storm" that comes into your experience, instead of looking for something with which to stop it, stand there and say, "Be not afraid. It is I." *I,* God, appearing as individual consciousness must be the law unto storms, winds, waves, volcanoes, or even atomic bombs.

In the Infinite Way, we are withdrawing all power and presence from the external world, whether it be in dollars, loaves, fishes, storms, sin, or disease, and we are putting that power where it belongs—in God, appearing as my individual consciousness and your individual consciousness. That *I,* that *I* that I am, is the law unto every storm.

When the people therefore saw that Jesus was not there, neither his disciples, they also took shipping, and came to Capernaum, seeking for Jesus.

And when they had found him on the other side of the sea, they said unto him, Rabbi, when camest thou hither?

Jesus answered them and said, Verily, verily, I say unto you, Ye seek me, not because ye saw the miracles, but because ye did eat of the loaves, and were filled.[18]

Yes, they came again for bread, but did they see the miracle? Did they see that it was consciousness that produced bread? Were they interested in that? No, they were interested only in getting more bread and more fish. Their attention was centered on the things of the world, on hating, loving, fearing, and desiring the things of the world.

Achieve Spiritual Consciousness

This leads up to the statement: "Take no thought for your life, what ye shall eat; neither for the body, what ye shall put on."[19] There is no use in our being fed by the great Master and then coming back tomorrow to be fed all over again. When you have witnessed a healing, do you say: "Now tell me the secret; tell me what the miracle is. I do not want to see *effects;* I must see the miracle at work"?

Please watch this point. Watch that your senses do not become hypnotized by the magnitude of the demonstration, so that you forget to ask: "What is the miracle of the demonstration? What is the cause of the demonstration?" We must let God, the consciousness of our being, be the measure of our demonstration. Our consciousness, being infinite, must appear as infinite loaves and fishes, as an infinite amount of dollars, as infinite home, infinite activity.

And now we come to the essence of our work. After Jesus answered them, "Ye seek me, not because ye saw the miracles," we read further:

> Labor not for the meat which perisheth, but for that meat which endureth unto everlasting life, which the Son of man shall give unto you. . . .[20]

Do not labor, do not study, do not meditate or treat, *for an effect.* Do not live in the world of thought and things. Labor for the state of consciousness which will bring forth the eternality of your mind and body and purse, of your home, family life, and human relationships, as well as of national and international affairs.

Spiritual consciousness does not put its value in "the meat which perisheth." It puts its value in the consciousness which is the law of life, and which becomes the *form* of "the meat which perisheth." Jesus did not say that we should not have that meat. He said that the Son of man will give you the true meat, and it is for that meat that we should strive—for that state of consciousness.

The purpose of our work is the revelation of a new type of man, the revelation within our own being of the spiritual man we really are. Most of us are not happy with what we see and with what we seem to be. We shall never be happy until we get back to the man that we really are. Then the struggle between the Spirit and the flesh, which has been going on throughout all time, will come to an end. The end of this struggle and the opening of consciousness to spiritual development became more than a vague hope when spiritual teachers began to introduce God as a seven-day-a-week possibility—in fact, as a seven-day-a-week necessity. The world is asking now for a new type of man in whose consciousness there is no war, nor anything which breeds war. And that truly is a miracle!

Then said they unto him, What shall we do, that we might work the works of God?

Jesus answered and said unto them, This is the work of God, that ye believe on him whom he hath sent.[21]

That is one of the greatest statements in the Bible: ". . . that ye believe on him whom he hath sent." Whom hath He sent? Himself as your consciousness and as mine! God individualized as the Son! God has sent Himself into manifestation as you and as me. You must learn to believe in your own consciousness as being the consciousness of God appearing as your own consciousness. That is how you will learn to do the works of God. It is not wrong to do those works, because he said that we could do them. He might have said, "You poor little souls!" But he said: " . . . that ye believe on him whom he hath sent." Believe that the divine, infinite Consciousness, called God, has been sent into the world as your consciousness.

Flesh and blood cannot inherit the kingdom of God, and because you have dealt with flesh and blood throughout your own experience, you have not entered into heaven. You must now turn from all concern over flesh and blood and begin to understand "whom he hath sent." When you begin to believe, really and truly believe, that God is the consciousness of you, that all issues come from the divine consciousness of you, and not from outside, not from effect, you will be on the first rung of the ladder of spiritual unfoldment.

They said therefore unto him, What sign shewest thou then, that we may see, and believe thee? what dost thou work?

Our fathers did eat manna in the desert; as it is written, He gave them bread from heaven to eat.

Then Jesus said unto them, Verily, verily, I say unto you, Moses gave you not that bread from heaven; but my Father giveth you the true bread from heaven.

For the bread of God is he which cometh down from heaven, and giveth life unto the world.[22]

What is that *he?* Is it a man, or is it your consciousness? It is divine Consciousness appearing as your individual consciousness, giving life unto your body, your position, your home. The bread of God is infinite, divine Consciousness appearing as your individual consciousness—God unfolding, revealing, and disclosing Itself as your individual being. When you know that, you really can believe on It, and trust that every issue of life will come forth—all supply, all peace, all dominion.

Then said they unto him, Lord, evermore give us this bread.

And Jesus said unto them, I am the bread of life: he that cometh to me shall never hunger; and he that believeth on me shall never thirst.[23]

The world thinks that *me* means a man named Jesus Christ, who lived two thousand years ago. But that *me,* that *I,* is God, the infinite Ego, appearing as individual ego. "I am the bread of life"; and, therefore, the place whereon I stand is holy ground because *I* am there. Isn't that a tremendous thing! Spiritual consciousness individualizes Itself as you! The world has been saying Jesus Christ is, or was that, but how can it help us if only Jesus is that, and I am not that *I?*

But I said unto you, That ye also have seen me, and believe not.

All that the Father giveth me shall come to me; and him that cometh to me I will in no wise cast out.

For I came down from heaven, not to do mine own will, but the will of him that sent me. [24]

Can you not see that this is true of us, that our only purpose is to do the "will of him that sent me"? Nobody could be attracted to a person, now or two thousand years ago, for some kind of a personal message he had of his own. Unless you can see, not only that I, the writer of these words, came to do "the will of him that sent me," but that such is your function in life, as well, you will have missed the point of all this work.

The Purpose of Life

This leads us to one of the greatest subjects in the world: For what purpose were we born? It cannot be that we came to this experience merely for the purpose of making a living, doing housework, bookkeeping, or whatever our lot in life may be, all for the privilege, at last, of laying ourselves down to die. Doing only those things means that we have not yet found our destiny.

The moment, however, that you identify God, infinite Consciousness, as your individual consciousness, you will break through your environment, regardless of how limited it may seem to be. The urge comes: "I must find my purpose on earth." There is a high purpose here for all of us. "Is it not written in your law . . . Ye are gods?"[25] Always the Master was trying to lift up this false sense of selfhood to its true identity, God, which you are. Jesus was telling his people to be just what he was.

~20~

And this is the will of him that sent me, that every one which seeth the Son, and believeth on him, may have everlasting life. . . . [26]

If you can actually see, or feel, God working through some person, then, you must recognize that what is true of him must be true of you, because his experience was like yours until the Spirit touched him. The purpose of spiritual truth is to raise you up into a realization of your true identity. If you can believe that you have witnessed a trace of spiritual or God consciousness emanating from any spiritual teacher, then you are believing that "the Son" is in him and the minute that you believe that "the Son" is in him, you yourself are saved. You are lifted up so that you know what is true of him is true of your own identity. Otherwise it would not be true at all. God is no respecter of persons. Look back on the history of all spiritual leaders and you will discover that something happened in their housewifely or clerkly minds, which awakened them to the fact of the Christ as their own being, to the fact of their own being as "the Son."

And this is the will of him that sent me, that every one which seeth the Son, and believeth on him, may have everlasting life: and I will raise him up at the last day. [27]

That realization of "the Son" within will raise up your own individual being to that point where you can agree that anything that has ever been true of the spiritual leaders of the past, is the truth about you, because it is the same *I* appearing as you and as me.

The Jews then murmured at him, because he said, I am the bread which came down from heaven. [28]

How human beings hate to hear that! How it antagonizes them to hear someone say, "I have something of God in me. I am the very presence of God." They resent this because they feel that someone is setting himself up as greater or as separate from the rest of them, not understanding that he is only setting forth a principle for everyone to adopt.

And they said, Is not this Jesus, the son of Joseph, whose father and mother we know? how is it then that he saith, I came down from heaven?

Jesus therefore answered and said unto them, Murmur not among yourselves.

No man can come to me, except the Father which hath sent me draw him: and I will raise him up at the last day.

It is written in the prophets, And they shall be all taught of God.[29]

Do you see that? Jesus sets himself up and glorifies the Christ in him, but then he turns about and says: "And they shall be all taught of God."[30] Again, he is minimizing the human selfhood.

The purpose of our study is that God may reveal Itself as our individual consciousness: I am the Word become flesh. The beginning of wisdom is when we draw our attention away from the outer world, from the world of effect or appearance, and begin to realize that power is not in it, but in me. All power is given unto me. *I* have dominion over everything that appears in the world of effect.

Instead of giving treatments, let us see if we cannot smile, at least inwardly—not openly, in a way to offend or appear to minimize someone's suffering, but inwardly smile—in the sense of, "Yes, but I know that there is no power in the appearance. The power is in me, in the consciousness of the individual, whether the individual is this one or that one. God, the consciousness of any individual is the power. I no longer hate, fear, or love what appears outside, or what mortal man or mortal effect can do to me." Stop giving power to numbers, to loaves and fishes, because they have no power. *"I* am the power." God, the divine Consciousness, must appear as my infinite spiritual supply, as my infinite spiritual body.

Importance of the State of Consciousness of the Practitioner

When you turn to a practitioner for help, what do you think it is that meets the need? Have you any idea at all why, how, or through what process, you expect the healing? Is it a blind faith, a confidence in the practitioner, or a confidence in God? Or do you recognize that the healing is done by the consciousness of the practitioner? When you ask a practitioner for help, that help comes because the practitioner has arrived at that state of consciousness wherein evil, or error, of any name or nature has lost its power.

If you ask for help from someone who believes that a pain is something to be afraid of, or that error is something to hate or to fear, you will not have a healing. But when you ask for help from a practitioner who has no fear of germs, infection, or contagion—who knows that germs, infection, or contagion do not exist as power, but merely as effects—you will have a very quick healing. It is the state of consciousness of the practitioner which heals.

Someone may ask, "Where is God in all that?" In consciousness, of course. That is where God is. God is that consciousness which actually knows that there is nothing opposed to It. God is that state of the practitioner's consciousness which neither fears, hates, nor loves error in any form: Then, and only then is the practitioner capable of healing.

The practitioner who is afraid of disease, or disgusted with this or that form of sin, or who criticizes or condemns the alcoholic or the sensualist, is not evidencing a state of healing consciousness. The state of consciousness of the practitioner is the healing agency in just the proportion that his state of consciousness has lost its fear, hate, or love of error of every name and nature. If we fear a certain condition and believe that it has power to kill, we cannot heal. And let us understand right now that there is no God sitting around waiting to take up the job for us.

God is infinite divine consciousness, in which there is no sin, disease, or death. That is the practitioner's state of consciousness insofar as this truth is recognized. No one has fully overcome the belief that there is power and presence in matter, although Jesus accomplished it more than all others.

There is another thing to be considered at this point. You may wonder why it is that you can go to a practitioner one day and have an instantaneous healing, and then, the very next time, you may have to go back four or five times before the healing comes forth. That is because the practitioner, in that particular moment of the instantaneous healing, is in such a high state of consciousness that he is entertaining neither hate, fear, nor love for the outer appearance. With the next call for help, the mesmeric suggestions of the world, coming to him through radio or newspaper headlines, or because of family troubles, may have dragged him down from that high state of consciousness.

The economic system under which we are living today is not the same as it was in Jesus' time. Then, it was possible for Jesus to pick up his white robe and go up to the mountain top for forty days, and then later come back and heal the multitudes. If we could do that today, we, too, might heal the multitudes. But the average practitioner cannot do that. As a matter of fact, the patients, themselves, are partly responsible for this state of affairs. They tend to resent it when the practitioner is not available when they want him. They want to be able to reach him twenty-four hours a day, seven days a week, and therefore, in a measure, they help to block these instantaneous healings. They do not permit the practitioner to remain at the height of consciousness necessary to bring them about. A practitioner would do far better work if he could go away, at frequent intervals, for two or three days at a time.

There is no mystery or miracle about healing. Healing is the direct result of the consciousness of the one to whom you turn. When you reach out for help, you reach out to the consciousness of the practitioner. If practitioners were always at the infinite-God-state of consciousness, then every time you reached out for help, you would have an instantaneous healing. It is only because we have not achieved that state of consciousness and do not maintain it that healings do not follow.

You will heal in proportion to your awareness of this truth: God, not your human thinking mind, is your divine consciousness. When you are called upon for help, turn instantly and unhesitatingly to your highest understanding, knowing that help is forthcoming in the degree of your realization of God as your individual consciousness, a consciousness which knows nothing about error in any form, and therefore, neither hates, fears, nor loves it.

In proportion as you study, in proportion as you meditate, Truth, or God, is disclosing and revealing Itself as your individual consciousness.

~2~

PEACE

Peace I leave with you, my peace I give unto you:
not as the world giveth, give I unto you. Let not your
heart be troubled, neither let it be afraid.

John 14:27

My[*] peace, the peace of Christ! More healings have
been brought about through absolute silence than
through all the arguments metaphysicians have thought
up in the whole history of the world. When you are
called upon for help, sit down and get at peace. Think
no thoughts; just sit and wait. Wait. Be patient, and wait
for the peace of the Christ to descend upon you. In that
moment of peace, without a word, you will witness
healing.

The only value a treatment has is to lift us to a point
or place in consciousness where we are ready for
spiritual consciousness to unfold. We are now in a
different position from the one in which we found
ourselves, when we were functioning with treatments.
We have come to that place in consciousness where we
are ready for the next higher step. Even if mental
argument, affirmation, and denial were necessary to us
in the early days of our work, we can now leave such
forms alone.

---

[*] The word "My," italicized, refers to God.

Learn to sit down and relax. Whether the case is sin, disease, death, or unemployment; whether or not it is serious, sit down and relax. Do not try to "handle" it. Do not try to "work" on it. Do not try to "treat" it. Sit back and, in silence, create a kind of vacuum for God, for the Christ, to rush in. Sit down and relinquish the thought that the human mind is a healer: Christ is the healer. The essence of the whole work we are doing is this: God is. God is, so let God work in us and through us to Its own end, and as Its own creation. Instead of continuing to use the words, God, God, God, let the actual realization of God do the work, since God is.

"My peace I give unto you: not as the world giveth."[1] The world can give us a certain kind of peace. It can give us a lack of noise, a quiet country place, or an ocean trip. That is the peace that the world can give. People travel to far places, but they travel with themselves, and they return home with themselves. We cannot, any of us, get away from ourselves. If we have a problem, we take it with us, wherever we go.

We must stop all such futile efforts. The human mind is not the Christ. For many years, mental efforts have been tried. The words of the Bible are, "My thoughts are not your thoughts, neither are your ways my ways."[2] What good, then, is all this "thinking" that we have been doing? The truth of the matter is that the human mind plays no part in any healing. The only factor in spiritual healing work is the Christ. Spiritual healing means that healing which comes from one's realized Christ consciousness, rather than from mental argument or external means, such as medicine or surgery. "My peace I give unto you." In that peace that "passeth understanding," in that quiet, in that stillness, the peace of God, the power of God is made manifest, and it does the work.

In our work, many people seem to come, wanting only loaves and fishes, instead of seeking for God Itself. With that we need not be concerned. We are not to be concerned with what they appear to want. We just "sing our song." Those who can receive it, will; others may not be ready. You will find that more healings take place through a smile, through the simple recognition of the presence of God, than will ever take place through any mental striving; and they will be purer, sweeter, and more lasting healings because they will be the descent of the Holy Ghost, the Christ, Itself, coming into consciousness and dispelling the errors of sense.

Peace: A State of Non-Resistance to Error

Just what is required to "walk on the waters," to dispel the storm? Is it some mental argument, denial, or affirmation? All that Jesus said to the storm was: "Peace, be still."[3] That was all—just, "Peace, be still." Everyone who has done healing work knows that the healing has taken place when that sense of peace, that realization of the Christ, has been experienced. He may not know how, or why; but let me tell you the how and the why of it. It is because the state of consciousness of the practitioner in that peace did not fight, oppose, or resist the error or claim. That is the reason for the healing.

This, I learned through an actual experience in the first year of my practice. A man, suffering from tuberculosis, was brought to my office by a friend of his. When I agreed to help him, he mentioned the difficulty he had in eating solid food because of pyorrhoea and asked for some help for this condition, also. I assured him that I would help him with that, too, but in my youthful enthusiasm, I forgot all about the pyorrhoea. However, the following morning, he called and said, "What have you done to me? I have just spent five minutes with a stiff tooth-brush having a wonderful time and I could not move my teeth."

That gave me something to think about. It was my first experience with "forgetting" something; but my second experience was to come soon after, when a telephone call came for help for a severe headache. The patient who was in my office at the time the call came recognized the urgency of the call and at once proceeded to leave. Before she had reached the door, the telephone rang again, and the young woman who had been suffering from the headache reported that the pain had disappeared. It had been an instantaneous healing.

Such things do not happen to a person in this work without causing him to question, "How?" Either these things are accidents, isolated instances which might have happened anyway, or they reveal a principle. As I studied and observed closely any and everything which would help to reveal the secret, I learned this: Healing is not brought about by the human mind; it is done by a state of consciousness imbued with the Christ. Christ consciousness is the understanding that disease does not exist as a reality and does not have to be fought. The very act of "forgetting" shows that the practitioner does not take it too seriously.

The one who is showing forth the Christ light, the Christ healing light, is the one who is not making a reality of error, is not fighting it; but, in a peaceful recognition of the fact that God is the life of individual being, quietly realizes, "Not by might, nor by power, but my Spirit."[4] One person, sitting in a room in silence, in a state of receptivity, can have that silence and that peace which he experiences felt by a roomful of people. How then can we measure what can happen with little groups scattered around the world, all maintaining this great power of silence?

If your consciousness is imbued with silence, with peace, then it is imbued with power. Healing takes place through the consciousness of the practitioner. The state of your consciousness will determine the healing of those who come to you, not that the healing power is yours as a person. The healing power is the presence of God, the Spirit of God, appearing as individual consciousness. You do not have this healing power unless you have a consciousness that is at-one with divine Love, a consciousness that is at-one with the peace "which passeth all understanding."[5]

When you go out into the business world, if you really want to be successful—if you want to sell something, buy something, or bring to consummation any kind of business transaction—do as you do with healing: Go with peace in your consciousness. Do not go out with a fearful or doubting consciousness, or with a fretful consciousness; or you will impart this state of your consciousness to the one with whom you do business, and he, too, will feel it. Go with this silence in your heart; go in a state of peace. If necessary, before making your business call, go off somewhere for a minute or two, sit down, and get that sense of peace before you start out. Then see what that sense of peace will do; see what it has already done. The state of peace in your consciousness is a state of receptivity.

Peace: The Experience of God

Ultimately, we are going to learn the greatest of all secrets—the secret that hitherto has been known only to a very few—the secret of what God is. If we study the scriptures, if we study the philosophies and religious teachings of the world, we are likely to come to the conclusion that God is something very far-off, something that is very seldom contacted, and something that very seldom answers prayer in accordance with our wishes, needs, or desires. Because the world has no knowledge of what God is, it keeps on, generation after generation, praying for world peace and not achieving it, praying for individual prosperity and not achieving it, praying for life, health, immortality, and yet not achieving them.

If we are Christians, we should at least know *where* God is, because Jesus told us that "the kingdom of God is within you."[6] That alone would have been a wonderful foundation, if only we had believed it. If our fathers, grandfathers, and others who preceded us had spent the past two thousand years seeking the "kingdom of God within," then, by this time, it would have been found and made manifest. Instead, all the generations which have preceded us, have turned to some master on a platform, or have turned their eyes up to the skies, or have looked in every direction except the one where they were told to look—within. The time has come, in this century, for us to begin looking for that kingdom within our own being, for that is where we shall find God. Although I can tell you this, you, yourself, will have to have it revealed to you from within your own being. Then, you will find that God is life eternal and God is infinite consciousness. But you will find, also, one

~32~

thing more than that. You will find that this divine, universal Consciousness is manifesting Itself as your individual consciousness so that, ultimately, you will be able to say, "I and my Father are one."

We must know the nature of God and we must *experience* God. We should not go on for the next ten years as we have been doing up to now, just talking about God: The time has now come when *we must experience God.* Let us not pass lightly over this part of the teaching, because it is the most important part of it all. We must see God while we are yet in the flesh, and that means you and me, individually, here and now, without waiting to die. We must experience God through our periods of silence, our periods of peace.

Each time you sit down, think of the statement of the Master: "Peace I leave with you, my peace I give unto you"[7]–the peace that passeth understanding. Let yourself be enveloped with that peace. You will find the presence of God in that peace, and in that presence of God you will find power, joy, dominion, healing–healing not only for yourself, but for all those who have brought themselves within the atmosphere of your thought.

In the old method of metaphysical practice, the first thing we did when a problem was brought to us was to "answer it back," to think up some wise saying, some metaphysical or scriptural statement in some form or other, and quickly to affirm or to deny it. We were always denying some error and affirming some truth. In this new approach, we are not going to affirm, and we are not going to deny. We are going to sit quietly, achieve a sense of peace, and let that sense of peace do the work. We are going to prove that it is not the action of the human mind that heals.

You see, the danger of believing that your affirmation or denial is necessary, or that you have to think some kind of a thought, is that if you were in a position where you could not think, you would be without hope. But that could never be true, because so long as God is present, that is all that is necessary. When a thought is unfolded to us from within, however, that is an entirely different thing. That is a divine revelation of God, announcing the presence and the power of God. It is for that very reason that we spend so much time developing "the listening ear," the state of receptivity.

Begin now to change your old basis of treatment. If necessary, do it drastically; do it by forcing yourself to take no thought. I am asking you to come into a higher consciousness of the presence of God, a consciousness higher than that which you can attain through the action of the human mind. Let us move a step higher into that state of consciousness in which we would be if we were students of Jesus, who said: "Take no thought for your life, what ye shall eat, . . . or what ye shall drink, . . . your Father knoweth that ye have need of these things. . . . Consider the lilies, how they grow: they toil not, they spin not; and yet I say unto you, that Solomon in all his glory was not arrayed like one of these."[8]

So it is with us. Let us remember to adopt for ourselves that peaceful attitude of assurance and confidence, which fills us with the peace and the power of God. That consciousness is the very presence and power of God, Itself. When we are not thinking or struggling with thought, when we are not fighting error, our consciousness is the presence and power of God. This divine Consciousness is not really in effect—is not really effective—so long as the human mind is moving around in a circle. It is true that you cannot ever get away from the presence of God, but you do not benefit by It in such a state. You benefit only in the degree that peace descends upon you.

Paul experienced this peace as the descent of the Holy Ghost, as the Spirit of God in man. These are terms used to describe what appears to us when we are not thinking, when the only thoughts filling our consciousness are God's thoughts. In the silence, God fills our consciousness far more than when any thinking of ours is taking place. It is hard for us to imagine this state of being because we are so used to the idea that we must be thinking, or that we must be holding a thought. That is not true. If we could have silence for the space of half an hour, true silence, we would find ourselves in heaven. Silence is God in action. Therefore, when a problem confronts us, whether our own or another's, let us sit down and find that silence, and then let the solution appear.

Suppose that someone comes to us today with a problem. The problem may be one of unemployment, a sinful habit, or a state of ill health. Instead of refuting it, let us look through it in the realization that it exists only as an appearance. With "the listening ear" say, "All right, Father, throw the light on it, so that I may see it as it is." Then, watch what that kind of a treatment will do for you. In other words, when we see railroad tracks coming together, instead of asking, "Now what must I do to separate those tracks?" let us say, "Father, show me those tracks as they really are." Then we do not have to think about it any more.

Do not try to improve a person, or his health. Do not accept into your consciousness the thought that there is a person in ill health. Sit in a state of receptivity, relaxed, in a state of silence, a state of peace. Let that peace permeate your whole being, and when you have accomplished that, sit with a listening attitude, and watch the light dispel the darkness, watch intelligence dispel ignorance. Instead of your being the healer, you are a witness watching this state of peace do the healing. Be a beholder of the activity of the Christ, or God. Watch It work in you, and through you, and ultimately, *as* you.

"Though I speak with the tongues of men and of angels, and have not charity,"[9]–have not love, it availeth nothing. It would not make any difference how wonderful my speech, how marvelous the statements of truth which roll off my tongue. If these statements and this speech are not imbued with a sense of God's allness, they will be of no avail in the healing ministry. It is not the speech; it is not the letter of truth which is important: It is the degree in which the consciousness of the practitioner is imbued with an understanding of God as love and life; the degree in which the practitioner has lost the ability to fear, to hate, or to love error of every kind.

We read in John: "Not that any man hath seen the Father, save he which is of God, he hath seen the Father."[10] There is the crux of the whole matter. No mortal, nor any human being, can see God or know God. Only the Son of God, the Christ consciousness of you and of me, can ever witness and behold the presence of God. In other words, it is not our human mentality that will know God. Never with the human mind shall we see or know or understand God or spiritual living. But the Son of God, the Christ consciousness, our spiritual sense, can behold God.

A Developed Spiritual Sense Is Requisite

There is the heart of the Christ teaching. And that is where the human world has failed—trying to know God through thinking, trying to know God with the intellect, trying to "explain" God. It cannot be done. God is discerned only through spiritual sense. Only through a developed spiritual sense can you and I, individually, discern truth, the things of truth, and the formations of truth—the spiritual universe. We develop that spiritual sense in many ways: through our reading of metaphysical and scriptural literature; through teaching and being taught spiritual living; through association with people who are on the same path. Being together in one place, of one mind, develops that spiritual sense, which is called "the mind that was in Christ Jesus." Paul called it, "the Christ that liveth in me." In most cases it is a *developed* sense, and we must *consciously* develop it.

You can help to bring about the realization of God by acknowledging God throughout the day, and once or twice during the night. Realize God as the center, the reality, of your being. Realize God as the mind and Soul of you, functioning as your individual being.

I am the living bread which came down from heaven: if any man eat of this bread, he shall live for ever: and the bread that I will give is my flesh, which I will give for the life of the world.[11]

This bread, which is understanding, is the Word made flesh. As you, through the human mind, behold your body, you are beholding only the mortal and material concept of body, and that is all that you will ever behold with the human mind. But, through the development of this *I* which I am, this Father consciousness or Christ consciousness, you learn to look out on the universe through spiritual sense, and you, ultimately, begin to see the "body not made with hands, eternal in the heavens." That was John's vision of the Christ, his vision of heaven, while yet on this earth, while he was right here, walking, talking, and moving about among his people. He saw what no human brain or human eye can ever see. He saw the temple not made with hands; he saw the spiritual universe, the spiritual body. That is what you will behold when, instead of using thoughts, you become a state of silence, a state of peace. When you have felt that divine Reality, then you have seen the temple not made with hands, that body which is life eternal.

Then Jesus said unto them, Verily, verily, I say unto you, Except ye eat the flesh of the Son of man, and drink his blood, ye have no life in you.[12]

That, again, is but the Christ revealing Itself. Unless you eat and drink, unless you absorb, unless you realize, unless you see the temple not made with hands, you will not have life eternal. To eat and to drink means to take in, to absorb, to realize. The more you look out on the world through human reasoning, through human thinking, the more you have of a fleshly body which dies somewhere between sixty and a hundred years of age. But the more you take in, that is, the more you carry in your consciousness this truth of being, the truth about God and God's creation, the more will you manifest intelligence and life as long as you are using this body.

Many therefore of his disciples, when they heard *this,* said, This is an hard saying; who can hear it?

When Jesus knew in himself that his disciples murmured at it, he said unto them, Doth this offend you?[13]

The human mind is always offended at truth because truth is a reversal of everything that the human mind knows. Imagine saying to the human mind that when it is still and doing nothing, great and wondrous works of healing can be accomplished! That is an insult to the human mind. Think of saying to the man who prides himself on his intellect that all of his mental gyrations will not do as much for him as one moment of silence will do!

It is the spirit that quickeneth; the flesh profiteth nothing: the words that I speak unto you, *they* are spirit and *they* are life.
But there are some of you that believe not.[14]

What was it they could not believe? It was that the Spirit quickeneth and not the flesh, that it is the silence, the peace, that really does the work, and not the mental gymnastics, not what is learned in books or through the intellect. We, like the disciples, are not doing too well, either; we are not making such great progress. Today, just as in Jesus' time, the human mind is offended; it feels itself rebuked at the suggestion that there is a Spirit which works without words or thoughts, that there is a Spirit in man which can lift him up and guide him through life, and can still all the storms of life without his thinking a thought, saying a word, or giving a treatment.

But there are some of you that believe not. For Jesus knew from the beginning who they were that believed not, and who should betray him.
And he said, Therefore said I unto you, that no man can come unto me, except it were given unto him of my Father.[15]

And what happened?

> From that *time* many of his disciples went back, and walked no more with him.[16]

Is it strange that so few, even in this day, can grasp the great fact that it is the Spirit which quickeneth, that there is a Spirit in man that does the mighty works of healing and regenerating? The human mind takes offence when we try to give it up.

> The world cannot hate you; but me it hateth, because I testify of it, that the works thereof are evil.[17]

The world will never hate anyone who uses the world's weapons, or who uses accredited and accepted forms of activity. The world hates only those who say that all that is unnecessary, that there is a higher power, the power of Spirit. It is then that persecution sets in, not that any persecution is necessary. Today, we are learning to let the impersonal Christ absorb all the persecution, instead of allowing our human selves to take it on. We accept persecution by believing that the message we are presenting is "my" particular message, "my" particular truth. Instead, we should realize: "This is not my truth, but the Christ truth, and if you are going to hate anything, hate it, and not me. I am merely showing forth what the Master gave of the Christ teaching of the presence and the power of That which is invisible to human sense, of That which is the state of your own being, the divine Consciousness of your own being, the Comforter which is within you. If the world wants to hate that truth, let it do so." That is the secret of the Master, that my peace "passeth all understanding,"[18] and that peace is power.

The Inner Meaning of the Temptations

Then was Jesus led up of the spirit in the wilderness to be tempted of the devil.

And when he had fasted forty days and forty nights, he was afterward an hungered.

And then the tempter came to him, he said, If thou be the Son of God, command that these stones be made bread.

But he answered and said, It is written, Man shall not live by bread alone, but by every word that proceedeth out of the mouth of God.[19]

Here we find the great inner meaning of the temptations. That passage is the cue to the principle of this entire teaching. The temptation was to demonstrate an *effect*, to demonstrate bread, to perform a miracle in the outer world, to center the thought and attention on the things of this world, that is, on the outer need. But the mind of Jesus knew that such is not the way of demonstration. The way of demonstration is this: "Since God is divine consciousness, and since consciousness is the substance and the activity of all form, then as long as I live and move and have my being as consciousness, all form will appear without my taking thought." And that was Jesus' answer to every temptation.

That must be your answer also. Instead of "working," that is, doing mental work, when any problem confronts you, remember that you have accepted the two great statements of the Master: "Take no thought for your life, what ye shall eat; neither for the body, what ye shall put on"[20]; and "Seek ye the kingdom of God; and all these things shall be added unto you."[21] When temptation comes to you to try to utilize this truth to secure a job, to perform a healing, or to do something in the outer realm, say with the Master:

I do not live by bread alone, but by every word that proceedeth out of the mouth of God. I do not live by outer demonstrations. They are the "added" things. They are the things that come to me of their own accord through my realization of God, the divine Consciousness, forever disclosing Itself as my individual consciousness. As long as divine consciousness is my consciousness, then It is the source of my supply, and I do not have to perform magic. I do not have to set up the personal "I" to be a demonstrator. The one I, the great I Am, is governing, maintaining, and sustaining Its own image and likeness. If, then, I try to perform a miracle, if, then, I try to make a demonstration; I am setting up an "I" apart from God; I am setting up a selfhood apart from God. God is forever maintaining Its own.

That is why the human mind makes trouble. That is why the human mind set up the prodigal, who went out into the world. He was not satisfied to live on the inheritance of his father, but wanted to go out and make his own way in the world. And you know where he ended up.

Then the devil taketh him up into the holy city, and setteth him on a pinnacle of the temple,
And saith unto him, If thou be the Son of God, cast thyself down: for it is written, He shall give his angels charge concerning thee . . . lest at any time thou dash thy foot against a stone.
Jesus said unto him, It is written again, Thou shalt not tempt the Lord thy God.[22]

If we have God, Itself, as our consciousness, do we need to produce angels, do we need to demonstrate "effects" of any kind to hold us up, to support us and help us? Do we need aught beside Him, or It? When we

look to anything but God, are we not becoming idola-
ters? Are we not looking for a "lesser than God" to bear
us up? And is not that the sin against the real God? Is
not that the sin against our own spiritual sense of life?
When we are tempted to turn to "man, whose breath is
in his nostrils," when we are tempted to rely on some
human form of God, even though it may appear to us as
an angel, let us remember Jesus' temptation. Have *I* any
need of angels? Have *I* need of any help? Have *I* need of
any lesser forms of help, even that of human thinking?

> Again, the devil taketh him up into an exceeding high moun-
> tain, and sheweth him all the kingdoms of the world, and the glory
> of them;
> And saith unto him, All these things will I give thee, if thou wilt
> fall down and worship me.
> Then saith Jesus unto him, Get thee hence, Satan: for it is
> written, Thou shalt worship the Lord thy God, and him only shalt
> thou serve.
> Then the devil leaveth him, and behold, angels came and
> ministered unto him.[23]

The temptation comes to all of us, at some time or
other, to turn away from our highest sense of Soul, so
that we can improve our lot, tempting us to help the
situation by coming down from our standpoint of
oneness to a lesser form of treatment, tempting us to
come down to a reliance on something separate and
apart from God. And that is where we shall have to
resist temptation, and learn to sit in silence, in that state
of peace that sees no power in the appearance. Since
God is the individuality of your consciousness and mine,
we need no other help than an awareness of that; we
need no lesser form of treatment; we need no human
help, not even in the form of mental help. We need only
the constant consciousness of God as our consciousness.

I began by saying that we must all come to the place of knowing what God is. I come back to that again now. God is the principle of this universe, but God is manifest as individual consciousness. Your individual consciousness is the principle or law unto your individual universe and experience. Your outer experience is determined by the degree in which you realize God—divine Law, divine Life—acting *as your individual consciousness*. It is still God, even when it is your individual consciousness, and this does not mean that each one of us is, or has, a separate God. It means that God is the infinite, indivisible consciousness of the individual, but it is still infinite, and is still all power.

As we walk or drive about, living, moving and having our being in the consciousness of this ever present God as our individual consciousness, how far are we ever away from God, or from the guidance, direction, and protection of God? When we know God to be the divine reality of our being, we know that God is very close—nearer than breathing, closer than hands and feet. That is the secret. It is not enough to know that God is life eternal. We must know it to the nth degree, as Jesus did, by realizing, "I am life eternal." He did not say, "God is the way." He said, "I am the way." In other words: "All that God is, I am; all that God has, I have because I and the Father are one."

When you want to help somebody, do you see that you cannot turn away from your own consciousness—God consciousness—to give that help? Rather, let your own consciousness be imbued with peace; let it be filled with the same confidence that Jesus demonstrated in the overcoming of the temptations. Too much do we neglect that story of the temptations.

Remember that Jesus was up on the mountain top, but he was there with his consciousness, not separate or apart from it; and remember, furthermore, he knew that his own consciousness was the source of all good.

Every one of you, at some time or other, is going to be called upon to help somebody. Some of you are going to be called upon to help many, and no lesson will be of greater value to you than what I am telling you now. Beginning today, at this very moment, remember: It is your consciousness that does the work for your family, for your business, for your home, for your body. It is not some far-off God. It is your own individual consciousness when your consciousness is imbued with silence and with peace. All you have to do, and all you will ever be called upon to do, is to achieve that sense of peace.

Do not wonder what great truth you ought to know. There are probably no greater truths in the world than those you already know; but there is one thing that you must practice and achieve and that is a state of peace within your own consciousness, coupled with the realization that it is your own consciousness which is the healing Christ. When we know that *we* have the mind "that was in Christ Jesus," then, we know that we *already* have that mind which is the healing Christ: We already have that state of peace which comes from the realization that error is not power—error is not a thing. In fact, *error isn't.* You do not have to fight it, or wrestle with it, or attempt to manacle it, or sit up all night to be sure that it does not overcome you. What you must do is to learn how to find your peace.

As you walk up and down the world with a sense of peace in your consciousness—and that sense of peace comes to you only in proportion to your realization that God *is* and error is *not*–as you achieve that sense of peace, you have the Christ consciousness. All that the Christ consciousness is, is your individual consciousness when you no longer fear or hate or love error of any name or nature.

We have not done the healing work that we should have done, and in nearly every case the reason is the same. We wonder when the mind of God is going to do something, or when divine Love is going to begin to work, or how we are to attain divine Love or the healing Spirit. And so we cannot and never will do the work that we should because the mind of God is your mind; divine Spirit is your spirit; divine Love is the love with which you are imbued. The state of consciousness which does the healing work is your own mind in a state of peace. If someone comes to you for help, it is your responsibility to arrive at that state of peace that "passeth all under-standing," and that state of peace becomes the "peace, be still" to error of every name and nature. When a person calls upon a practitioner for help, it is that practitioner's responsibility to "live and move and have his being" in this state of peace, and if he is not already in it, to attain it, so as to bring about the healing. When that consciousness reaches a state of peace, harmony, well-being, and confidence, it becomes the transparency for healing.

Your individual consciousness and mine, in a state of *transparency,* is God! God is the consciousness of the individual, and it is that which heals.

~3~

GOD REVEALING THE INFINITY OF BEING

The words of wise *men* are heard in quiet more than
the cry of him that ruleth among fools.
Ecclesiastes 9:17

We are surrounded at all times by what Scripture
calls "angels," which hover about us always. Within us
are those divine ideas or spiritual impulses which guide,
lead, and direct us, even though as human beings we are
not aware of them. As human beings, brought up with
the ordinary church experience or with no church at all,
we are not aware of the fact that we are constantly under
divine government, divine guidance. In reality we are
under the law of the Spirit of God, and under the spirit
of the law of God. In practice, we walk around like the
Prodigal, thinking, "I, of mine own self, am something
and I am going out into the world to make a name for
myself, to earn a living for myself, and to become
something great of and by myself." Thereby, we set up
a counterfeit identity and develop concern about the
health, wealth, success, and contacts of this counterfeit
identity. Yet, all the time, even though probably we have
never thought of it, we have been completely surrounded by an atmosphere of love and completely
enveloped in divine Being. As a matter of fact, we are
divine Being. We are the Father-consciousness Itself, but
we have walked about in the world, believing that

consciousness to be something small, finite, insignificant, and unimportant.

The purpose of this ministry is to bring us back to the Father's house, back to a consciousness of the presence and power of God. We are in this work but for one purpose—to be led back to the kingdom of our own consciousness in which God is manifested as divine wisdom, as divine love, as life, truth, permanence, immortality, and eternality.

Synonyms for God

For a moment, let us consider the synonyms for God, taking just a few with which we are familiar. We know God as infinite being, and therefore, we take each of the synonyms for God as representing the allness and wholeness of God. We do not separate God into synonyms and then say, "This synonym represents one quality or activity of God, and this synonym represents another quality or activity." We understand that every synonym represents the allness of God, although we may use a certain synonym in order to emphasize some particular quality or activity.

Let me illustrate this. God is infinite; therefore, God is immortality or eternal life. Since that is true, eternal life must be as infinite as God, and must include the activities and properties of incorporeal Spirit, divine love, and eternal substance. God is infinite; God is infinite being; God is Spirit; God is the substance of the universe. Therefore, since God is infinite, Spirit and substance must be infinite, and incorporeal Spirit embraces, includes, and externalizes all the activity of life, truth, love, Soul, principle, law, together with all the other synonyms for God which are found in Scripture.

Why, then, do we divide the word God into synonyms and use them interchangeably? It is for the same reason and in the same way that you may speak of my being a man, a husband, a father, a friend, a practitioner, a teacher, a lecturer, and a writer. But each one of these includes all the others. When you speak of me, for instance, as a teacher, you do so to emphasize one particular phase of my work, but this does not mean that you are not aware of my being all the other things, too. In the same way, when I think of you as a friend or as a student, I also think of you as a man, a woman, a mother, or a father. At least, in the back of my mind, I know that you are all those things, too. I cannot separate the "you" of you as a student from the "you" of you as a parent, husband, wife, or friend.

When we think of healing and of healing work, we turn to the word of God to bring out the divine allness of individual being. We turn to God to bring out—to disclose, to reveal, to unfold, to manifest—the allness of God, the allness of divine Being as your individual being. We do not want to bring out the harmony of your being in one area and lose sight of it in other areas, but rather, we bring out the allness of the divine Being as your individual being. We do this because we are not yet at that level of consciousness which does not occasionally require what we call treatment, and for that reason we make use of the synonyms for God.

Now we acknowledge that there are varying states and stages of consciousness. One person, coming into a metaphysical teaching, may come in on the level of a deeply religious consciousness. He comes into the fullness of understanding through first entertaining a clear idea of love, of God, of the Christ, of the Master, and of his disciples. Devotional religious love may predominate in his approach to the spiritual path.

But there are others to whom this would be unintelligible. These students understand God to be infinite intelligence; they are not interested in the devotional approach to God, and, oftentimes, not even in the word God. I have heard metaphysicians say, "Forget that word God. You use it too much." In the same way, another one of my friends was opposed to the term the Christ, and said, "Can't you think of something else for the Christ? Can't you say "the truth" or "the law"? I answered that I could, but that the Christ to me was something so personal, so still, and so sweet, that I would not want to give up that term.

To some students, divine Love might mean a great deal. Still another person might come in on the level of mind, and, in that case, his trend or his prayer would be more along the lines of realizing mind, manifest as idea, manifest as activity, manifest even as law. There are those who can only understand God as law, and they are very rigid about the idea that God is law.

It is not for us to judge as to whether anyone is "right" or "wrong." These various approaches to metaphysical work are merely degrees or different states of consciousness, and each one of us, according to his own background, environment, or pre-existence sees this work in a different light. One comes through devotion, one through mind, and one through principle. But if we are progressing, if we are understanding more and more of this work, we are coming to that place in consciousness where no treatment is ever necessary, and in that state we look out upon the world, beholding the perfection which underlies all appearances. Then we are not touched by any appearance. We know the appearance to be unreality, a false sense of the real, and we do not give a treatment. Yet no matter how far we progress in this work, there are times when we are called upon to think in terms of what the world might call a treatment, and that is where the use of the synonyms for God comes in.

In treatment in its highest sense, we turn to the principle: We turn to God. We touch and make contact with that, and all of a sudden, we feel the divine life-energy flowing through. That is all there is to treatment. Then, after we have made the contact, usually word comes that the patient is healed or improved. If he is not completely healed, we make the contact again, and again. Ultimately, he, himself, realizes his freedom and says: "Now I am healed, and I know it."

If we have difficulty in establishing that contact, if our own thought is not sufficiently clear to carry us immediately to the throne of God, then these synonyms serve a wonderful purpose. Let us suppose that we are confronted with a condition of illness where there seems to be a danger to life. Life is not in danger. That is only the appearance, for Life is never in danger. So, in turning to God as life, we think of life as immortality and eternality. We think of life as having no beginning and no ending. We see Life as the life of the universe, the life and the law, not only of individual man and woman, but of all that is appearing as the animal, vegetable, and mineral world. We see God as the life of the universe. We allow our thought to dwell on this idea of life eternal, life immortal, and we let any thoughts that come to us along this line unfold. When that has gone on for a while, and we finally feel we have come to an end of this contemplation, we just keep the listening ear open until we feel the truth. Then we can say, "Thank you, Father, it is done."

Another case may present itself to us, and this time it may be something with the appearance of paralysis, of inaction or overaction. In such a case, we may quickly think of mind as the instrument of God:

Mind is the source and seat of all action. Mind, as the instrument of God is the law unto all manifestation, unto all creation. Infinite Intelligence governs, maintains, and sustains Its ideas. Body, as idea, is a formation of mind, just as the reality underlying all formation is right idea. Without mind, there is no idea. Without idea, there is no mind, because there could not be mind without activity, and the activity of mind is idea. There cannot be paralyzed mind, or paralyzed idea. There can be only harmonious activity in mind, which is the instrument of infinite Intelligence and which expresses infinite activity.

In spiritual healing, always remember this: Never approach the healing work from the standpoint of disease or from the standpoint of the patient. Leave your patient out of it entirely. The moment a claim is presented as person or condition, drop it from your mind, then and there, and go to that word God. Drop all sense of man, of sin, of disease, of lack and limitation. If you find yourself struggling with these errors, trying to improve or change them, you will not bring about healing. Go to that word God as quickly as you can. Then, if you like, jump from God to one of the synonyms, and in that way work out from God.

Love Is the Basis of All Relationships

It is the same in any problem of human relationships. It may be the relationship between employer and employee, between husband and wife, between parent and child. But actually, in each and every situation, what we are dealing with is God. In all cases of human relationships, love is the only relationship there is, because God is love. Did you ever stop to think that there would be no relationships at all between human beings, if there were not love to cement that relationship? Whether the relationship is between parent and child, or whether it is between human beings and birds, beasts, or plants makes no difference. Love is the basis of all relationships.

Therefore, if the claim is that of a discordant relationship between people, let us turn immediately to the word God, and then quickly go from there to divine Love, emanating as an aura. Love is a permeating substance, a penetrating substance. Love is a cement, a uniting influence. Then come words like "unity," "oneness," "at-one-ment"–all properties of this divine Love.

Do you see that in thinking along these lines we have never thought about the persons involved, about the human beings in the picture and their worried or disturbed relationships? All we have thought about is Love and Its properties, Love and Its qualities, Love and Its influence, Love and Its omnipresence. By the time we have finished thinking about Love, the telephone should be ringing with someone at the other end telling us that there has been a reuniting.

These examples show us the reason for using synonyms for God. We are seeking merely to find the word that most closely fits the situation as it is presented to us in the human picture. Yet, all the time we are talking about Love, let us remember that Love is also divine intelligence, Love is also substance.

When we think of love, we cannot help going back to the ministry of the Master: "My peace I give unto you[1] ... Love the Lord thy God with all thy heart, and with all thy soul, and with all thy strength, and with all thy mind; and thy neighbor as thyself."[2] You will never stray far from the Christ while you are dealing with love, and you will never stray far from "Peace be still,"[3] while you are living with that word "love." In the same way, you will never get very far into sin, disease, or death, while your thought is being permeated with the consciousness of life eternal. Just go back to the Master, to *I*, to *I am*. Become so familiar with the teaching of the Master that no matter what situation arises, some of his very gentle, persistent statements immediately come to life: "I am the way, the truth and the life . . .[4] I am come that they might have life, and that they might have it more abundantly."[5]

Have you ever stopped to think how much time you spend trying to find some truth, or wishing that you might know some particular truth? You do not have to do that at all. If you can realize the Master's saying: "I am . . . the truth," then, you will have it all. "I am the truth!" And when you have that, you do not have to look for some truth which I already am.

Have you ever thought how much time you spend seeking love? It is time wasted because it is always to be found where you never think to look for it. It is within your own being: *I* am life, truth, and love. *I* am love. *I* am the only love there is in the world. I am all that God is; all that the Father hath is mine. Our mistake is that we look for love in or from some person. There we shall never find it–never. The love we find in a person is a counterfeit of love. We shall find love only when we discover it as the reality of our being.

In the same way, how often do we look to somebody for justice, for mercy, or gratitude. We cannot find these qualities in any person because they are not there to be found.

All these are qualities of your own being. If you do not find them within you, and if you do not find them very much in expression, do not look for them outside. But if once you do find that justice, mercy, kindness, benevolence, and gratitude are qualities of your own being, and that you are allowing them to come into full expression, then you will not look for them in anyone else, ever again. You will not have to, because they will be reflected back to you from the rest of the world, but always what is being reflected back to you will be the qualities of your own being.

Please remember this: You will never get anything from this world, except the quality of your own being. Therefore, anything which comes to you will come only by reflection. It is as if you stood in front of a mirror and saw whatever stands before the mirror. There is nothing in the mirror to be seen: What you see is your own selfhood reflected back to you.

This is a law and a principle. The quality, whatever its name or nature, is in our own being. When someone expresses it to us, he merely reflects our own being back to us. It is our own quality which has been reflected.

Never "Treat" a Person

I do not want to dwell too much on modes and methods of treatment, because I do not believe them to be too necessary at our stage of development. Yet I do recognize that in some small degree, treatment always will be necessary. We cannot completely overlook it. Therefore, in all my writings you will find some reference to treatment. These are enough to keep you on the path, and yet not allow you to sit upon a cloud and remain there without some resting place for your feet.

Now I want to explain one reason why we never treat a person, why we never give a treatment to any person. If anything in my writings has led to the belief that I would ever give a treatment to any person, let me correct that concept now. I have been in this work for twenty-eight years, and never have I given a treatment to anyone. Sometimes people say, "I got your treatment, and it was beautiful." That is impossible. I have never given a treatment to anyone, and I have never directed my thought to a person. I have never addressed the individual consciousness of any person. Never have I said, "You are spiritual; you are perfect; you are God's child." Never have I allowed the name of a patient to come into my thought while I was "treating." Never have I allowed the face, or thought, or outline of any face or body, to come into my treatment.

I do not, I cannot, give a treatment until the person asking for help is completely out of my thoughts. My treatment is based on lifting thought up to God and on eliminating any sense of person. I jump, as fast as I know how, up to the word God: I lift my thought over the person's head, not because God is up there, but because for me it eliminates personality and person, and then I am in God. Then I come out from God, and let flow out whatever truth I know about God—all the truth I know about God. I never connect it with any individual. And the reason is this: God is the only individual in the world. God is infinite individuality; God is the only place, the only person, the only power. God is the only reality. If I turned away from God, I would be treating an illusion.

Suppose I were to put your photograph in front of me, and having looked at it, decided that I did not like it; so I try to improve it by giving it a treatment. I could do that by touching it up with a little paint here, and a little more there. But after I have finished doing that, I would have only an improved photograph. It would not change you in the slightest degree. In the same way, if I gave you or your body a treatment, even if we patched it up and did something to it that would make you say, "It feels better," we still would have only an improved "illusion," an improved concept.

When I look at you, all I see is God. But I cannot see that with my physical eyes. All that I can see with those eyes is a very finite, mortal, material concept of God, appearing individually. Therefore, no matter what my eyes tell me about you, they do not testify truly. If they testify that you are sinning, sick, or dying, it is a lie. But if my eyes testify that you are beautiful, well, healthy, happy, and prosperous, that also is a lie. Those two opposites are but phases of the same belief–healthy or unhealthy, wealthy or not wealthy. If I want to know the truth about you, I must discern that through spiritual consciousness. Only spiritually, can I discern the reality of your being. But when I do discern that, I find God because God is the reality of your being. God is the eternal you.

If you do not believe this, go back to the New Testament and find what Jesus said about you and about me: "I am the way, the truth, and the life[6] . . . he that hath seen me hath seen the Father."[7] He was talking about himself, but he was also talking about you and about me. Of the "illusory" human self of him, he said: "I can of mine own self do nothing.[8] . . . My doctrine is not mine, but his that sent me[9] . . . If I bear witness of myself, my witness is not true."[10]

Jesus recognized that there is the Christ, the Son of God, *and* this body and form that the world was seeing and calling "Jesus." Of that form and concept, he said, in substance: "It can of itself do nothing; it is of itself nothing; if I speak of it as something, I speak a lie. But *I*, my message, which I am in my infinite, eternal being, that is God."

If I want to know the truth about you, there is no use looking at your form and trying to find it there, for that form cannot testify to truth. Only with my inner vision can I do this, that means with the inner spiritual light of the world which I am, *and which you are.* In that manner I can tabernacle with you; I can commune with you; I can be with you; and we can be friends unto eternity.

The minute we think in terms of the external appearance, we may have friends today, but those same friends may be our enemies tomorrow. It works out like that because in looking at people as they appear to be, we are dealing with a selfish sense of self, an egotistic sense of self, which is always saying, "I need this, and you have that." When we are on that level of life, we cannot behold each other as God made manifest. We cannot behold the Son of God with the outer senses. We cannot, in the outer world, behold the Son of God individually appearing.

When you see a person manifesting illness, poverty, sin, disease, or deformity, do not give that person a treatment. If you want to know the reality, close your outer eyes, and open your inner vision so that you can see that right where the false appearance seems to be, there is the Son of God, the manifestation of God, God consciousness individually unfolding, expressing, and revealing Its own infinite being. No matter of whom I am thinking, I have to think of God as the individual person—God, infinite, divine Consciousness, manifesting the infinity of Its own being as that individual person.

Our patient is healed long before we get all these words out of our mouths. It is not meant that we should learn words, and then use them in treatment. It is meant only that we should catch the significance of this idea that we, individually, are really divine Consciousness, disclosing, unfolding, revealing, manifesting, and expressing Itself *as* individual you and individual me, regardless of any appearance. All there is, is God being me and God being you, but always God being: God, infinite; God, eternal, immortal Life; God, incorporeal Spirit, Soul, divine Substance, infinite Intelligence. We go right to God and stay there.

Realize and *feel* within your being all that God is, but do not do it with words. You will only get tangled up. But this is the truth of being; this is the truth you must know, not only in order that you may be free, but that all who come to you may be free. Truth, itself, will not free the world. It is your knowing the truth that will do that, and the truth that you must know is not some truth about a human being, about a photograph, but the truth about God and you, the truth about God appearing as Its infinite, individual manifestation.

In knowing that truth, please be sure that you know this, too: You are not alone in this work. You are not alone on the street, or in your home, or in the airplane in the sky. You are not alone in peace, or in war. The symbols of God are all about you. God is always appearing in some kind of protective form, because God is not formless. God is always in the form of some divine idea. The divine Presence, the divine Being is sitting right on your shoulder. It is even closer; It is within your own consciousness, within the very being of you. If you will live in this spiritual life or in this light of Truth, you will always be consciously aware of God, if not of Him in the absolute sense, then in the form of a gentle thought, or a state of peace. There is always a peace surrounding us, if we open our consciousness to it; but we must learn to keep consciousness open to it.

The Infinite Way does not try to impart a mode or method of getting healthier or wealthier. Through this correct letter of truth, it shows you the truth of your own identity, the truth that God is your own identity. Its whole purpose is to open your consciousness to the conscious awareness of the presence of God in some particular form—as a matter of fact, in infinite form and in infinite variety, but in a form necessary to your development at this particular moment. We have to live so as to be conscious, continuously, of the divine presence of God in individual form, of a divine influence—angels—ever present in human consciousness. And this is God appearing as love, God appearing as life, God appearing as the very truth you seem to need at any given moment, God appearing as substance and supply.

The Spiritual Sense of Sharing

The only reason that you or I, individually, and the world, collectively, experience inharmony and discord in the form of sin, disease, and death is the belief that we are something other than God-being. That is the only reason we experience such things. The moment we realize that God is the reality of our being, we no longer need what anyone else has, and this ends all wars, all competition, all trickery, all dishonesty. Think how impossible it would be to realize that God is our mind, Soul, Spirit, supply, and then want anything that anyone has, except in the sense of sharing. And that very moment we come to realize God as the reality of our being, we can be as generous as we choose to be because we can feed the "five thousand."

There is no true sense of spirituality or of generosity except that which knows that whatever is pouring out is being poured out from the infinite storehouse called God. Any other sense of generosity or gratitude believes in a person as the source of it, and this results in that person's being set up as something great and generous. Real generosity, real sharing, and real gratitude come only with the understanding that whatever it is that I am imparting, whatever it is that I am sharing, whatever it is that I am giving, is of God. The only way in which I can accept anything from you, or from those of the world, is when I can realize that it is not coming from you or from them, but only *through* them. Therefore, when I accept anything from you—whether one dollar or one thousand dollars—and accept it in the sense that I am not taking it from you, and that you are not giving it to me, but that it is God revealing, expressing, and unfolding Itself, then that dollar, or that thousand dollars, will quickly be made up to you. You will find your storehouse quickly replenished.

You know very well that there is no truth reaching you from me. If there were, I would be left with a little less of truth when I finish this book, and you know that that is not true. I shall not be depleted in any sense. It works the other way. I do not feel that I have any the less of truth for having shared it, for truth is not my personal possession, and I do not have a barrel of it that is trickling out, the flow of which must be carefully guarded that it does not stop. You know, and I know, that Truth is spiritual, incorporeal, and that it is without limit.

Let us apply this same concept of supply and gratitude to any money we pay out of our pockets, whether for a bill of dry goods, or for a bill for metaphysical treatment. Try to feel that what you pay out does not leave you with that much less, because the whole thing is a liquidating flow, Spirit permeating all being. Unless you catch the vision that there is no matter, that there is no limitation, that there is no finiteness, that there is no such thing as a little piece of something or other called money—unless you catch that, you will be battling limitation all your life. The best way to grasp this idea is to think of supply as a synonym for Truth, as a synonym for God, or as the activity of God, and then forget such things as "mine" and "thine", and "how generous and thankful you should be."

See God as the Reality of All Relationships

Now that we are on the spiritual path, we are striving to live a spiritual life. We want it; we desire it; we hunger for it. But that is not enough: There is a price; there is a prerequisite for the spiritual life. We must overcome some of the natural tendencies of humanhood which are not natural to spiritual sense. We should give up the limited concept of religion which we have been entertaining, and begin to know, here and now, that real religion is the knowledge of God and of our true identity. Unless you see that true religion is the knowledge of God and the relationship of God and man, you will always be running from one church to another, from one teacher to another, or from one book to another. In living the spiritual life, may I assure you that you can live it very harmoniously whether in or out of church or organization, if you can understand the nature of God and the relationship between God and man.

Where your heart lies, there lies your treasure. In the religious world, there is but one place for your heart to be and that is in God and in the understanding of the relationship existing between God and God's creation. If you attain some degree of spiritual feeling, then you can go into any church at any time the door is open and sit there in peace and harmony and make your communion with God, the inner being of your Self. You have then caught the first step on the way to spiritual living—and that leads us to the second step.

After we have solved the problem of religious freedom, being in or out of the church, there still remains the problem of our relationship with those who constitute the members of the church. Our premise is that God, divine Consciousness, is unfolding, revealing, disclosing, and manifesting Itself as your individual being and as mine. Did you stop to think that we did not say, "unless you are a Jew," or "unless you are a Roman Catholic," or any other "unless"? The only "unless" that we know is that there is no spiritual living for you or for me unless we know that the life which is God is not only mine but yours also, no matter who or what we may be in the human picture.

If true religion is in our heart, if we are on the spiritual path, if we see God as the reality of our being and the being of all those with whom we come in contact, then we are certain to meet those who can be husband, wife, child, companion throughout all time and circumstance; and it will always be that one whom God has revealed to us and for us. It is said there are no marriages made in heaven, but this we do not believe. Marriages on earth may be made for earthly reasons, but there are marriages "made in heaven," and this occurs whenever an individual is truly on the spiritual path, living with God as his main concern and with companionship a secondary consideration. Then, will God disclose Itself, reveal Itself, *as* husband or wife. Under such circumstances, the marriage will be a rightful one; or God will reveal Itself as a rightful companionship, a rightful friendship, or a rightful neighbor. There is such a thing as a spiritual relationship between a man and woman. When I say that, I am not sitting on a cloud and saying that it cannot be manifested in a normal relationship.

The relationship that comes to us through spiritual attraction is not some intangible relationship out in space. It does not mean a relationship that cannot be understood by other people. It is the same kind of relationship as those which have existed since time began, only with a higher, cleaner, sweeter atmosphere about it. There is nothing gross or sensual about the relationship between friends, and in the same way, the marriage relationship can be normal, happy, and natural without coming down to the level of animalism. This is possible, and there actually are those who really and truly see God and the relationship of God to Its individual creation first, last, and always. That is our attitude on the spiritual path toward everyone we meet.

We must understand that we must be in the world but not of it where church and organization are concerned. The next step in our understanding is that we must be in the world but not of it in our relationships with each other—in all relationships from marriage to casual acquaintances. We must be in the world of these relationships and enjoy them all, but become attached to none.

Learn the Inner Meaning of Words

There is a further step. We must not use words in our religious life unless they mean something to us. Do not use the word God lightly. Do not use the word God unless you understand what you are talking about. The moment you say the word God and think that it means Jehovah on a cloud, or Jesus on the cross, you have not brought God into an understandable awareness in your daily life.

Take the word God into your heart, into your Soul, and pray the Father to reveal to you the real nature and character—the *is-ness* and the *what is-ness* of God—so that when you say God, you know as much of what you are talking about as when you use the word "mother" or "father." You understand the relationship of a mother to her child, and this relationship is the same regardless of the kind of mother to whom you are referring. From your experience, "mother" is different from the word "father," "brother," or "sister." There is no hidden mystery about these words. Each has its own meaning in your thought. Now you must make God as real to you as your friend, brother, mother, or father. Be sure that you gain an understanding of God, because without a knowledge of God, you cannot be on the spiritual path. You will never be on the spiritual path merely by talking about God, or by reading about God in books, hearing about God in lectures, or by taking instruction about God.

You will only know God when God reveals Itself to you within your own being. That can never happen unless you, yourself, bring it about. God will not force Itself on you. You, yourself, must make the decision to find the real meaning of the word God. When you succeed, God will have become an actual Presence and Power and you will not find yourself saying, "I know all about God, but I have never felt It or seen It; It is still a far-off God to me."

That must not happen to you. This instruction is not meant to enlighten you with a multitude of statements about truth. There are only three points comprising the letter of truth in this instruction, and these are: God; God individualized; and error as suggestion or world belief which must be rejected in order not to suffer from its effects. That is all. The purpose of this work is to keep lifting you in consciousness until you can say, "I know what God is." You must consciously develop this knowledge within your own being, for it comes from the depths of your being; and you must keep at it until you can live with God and commune with God, while driving a car, while walking, or shopping—until you can feel God flowing out.

I have said: Do not use the word God lightly. Make yourself come to know God. It is a most wonderful feeling, but it is more than a feeling. It is your life eternal. You are never going to have immortality or eternality—eternal life—until you know God, and not just some words about God.

The same is true with the word Christ. How that word is abused! The extent to which we use the word Christ without understanding the light, the power, the gentleness, the divinity of that Presence is sacrilegious. Christ is a reality. Christ is being. Christ is not a Jesus of two thousand years ago. Christ is the Spirit that animated Jesus beyond anything which any man has ever known—but not beyond that which can be known. We can go as far as Jesus went in this, and further. Did not he say, "Greater works than these shall he do?"[11]

In the manifestation and the development of the Christ, the realization of Christ as your own being, there is nothing to demonstrate. "Your Father knoweth that ye have need of these things.[12] . . . it is your Father's good pleasure to give you the kingdom."[13] Never be guilty of trying to demonstrate something, and still claim that you are on the spiritual path. You have nothing to demonstrate. There is a heavenly Father; there is a divine Consciousness; there is a guiding Influence in this world; and It is here on earth. It is *yours*. We have gone as far astray as the Prodigal. Get back to where you learn, in a spiritual way, the meaning of God's creation, unfolding and revealing Itself as a wonderful universe, and then you will have learned the secret: You are not a human being.

All healing is in the world of belief. All healing takes place in the Adam-dream. God knows nothing about it, because in the entire kingdom of God there never was a sin, a disease, or a death. That is why we misunderstand Jesus' mission in the world. If you believe the church's teachings, then God sent Jesus to heal the sick. But, actually, God knows nothing about sickness, sin, or death.

Jesus has a function in this world. It is to reveal the Christ of your being. That was his function two thousand years ago, and that is his function today—not to set up a man to worship or some individual to revere, but to reveal the Christ of your own being. Therefore, do not use the word Christ lightly. Go to God with it. Take it into your consciousness and pray the Father that light be given to you on the Christ, and the mind of Christ.

The same is true of prayer. We should not pray lightly, nor use the word "prayer" lightly. Prayer, in its spiritual sense, is our individual communion with God. When you think of it in that light, you will not ask God for anything; you will not petition Him for anything; you will not desire anything of God. In the gentleness, in the peace of your communion with God, you will find fulfilment. That is prayer.

Do not use these words glibly, as clichés. Do not use them as they have been used in some metaphysical literature, or even in the Bible. Go to the Father within you for your own interpretation. Our teaching cannot be a teaching of words. It must be a teaching of the revelation and the unfoldment of the Christ in individual consciousness.

A spiritual life can be developed only in proportion as we know the inner spiritual meanings of the words we are using; for example, the meaning of the word God, as God reveals It to you within your own being, in a language that you can understand and with a meaning that is intelligible to you, even if you cannot convey it to someone else. It is much better that you have a feeling of the meaning of God without the ability to express It, than that you can recite a whole page about God without feeling It and realizing It. Do not feel troubled because of your inability to voice what you know and think and feel about God, about the Christ, about truth, or about spirituality.

There exists within you a divine Reality that can not always be put into words. Lao-Tse said: "If you can define it, it is not God!" But that does not mean that you cannot know It and feel It and realize It. And this comes through your conscious communion with God, which is the purpose of our work. The ultimate of our work is when God and the individual blend into *one*—when there is no longer the individual as man, but there is only God voicing Itself, declaring Itself, disclosing, unfolding, and revealing Itself unto this universe.

~ 4 ~

SCIENCE OF CREATION

We never attempt anything without meditation. We never begin any work without going into the depths of our being to make conscious contact with God. We are one with God—"I and my Father are one"[1]—but that oneness is of no help to us, except in the degree of our realization of it. There must be a conscious awareness of our oneness. This does not mean merely declaring, "I and my Father are one," stating or affirming it while we are grabbing our hat and coat to rush downtown. Something happens to us when we go within and make the contact for that *feel* of the Presence. It is an experience as vibrant and alive as an electric contact.

In our humanhood, we are cut off from the Source. That is what constitutes humanhood: a selfhood apart from God, a selfhood separate from God. But humanhood is a dream. We are never really separate from God, even though the effect on us is the same as if we were. To rise above humanhood, that is, above the experiences of a human being and human events, it becomes necessary, actually, for us to feel that we have God within our own being—to make a God-contact.

For that reason, in all my writings you will find that attention is called to the necessity of beginning with this conscious awareness in the morning and continuing with it throughout the day until sleep comes at night, abiding constantly in the consciousness of the presence of God. Heretofore, we have for the most part, been satisfied to learn something of truth from a book, or to make some affirmations. From this time on, that will not suffice. At some time during the day and during the night, you must make this conscious contact with the inner Being, which we call God. Then, for the rest of the night, you can abide in that. But make that contact; make it a reality.

In proportion as you consciously make that contact, your life will be rebuilt. In proportion as you learn to turn within before undertaking anything, whether it is writing, cooking, speaking, shopping—regardless of what it may be—if you actually practice this turning within and making the contact, your outer experience will be permeated with the Spirit, with divine wisdom, with divine guidance, protection, safety, and security.

The human world finds safety and security in dollars, or in armaments. We find our safety and security in our contact with God. We find that contact manifesting itself outwardly in whatever form is necessary to our daily experience. It may appear outwardly as anything from dollar bills to houses or automobiles. But we take no thought for anything external. Our entire thought is on contacting this infinite Being, this infinite Reality, this divine Presence that is within us. Jesus called it, "the Father," and "the Father within." He told us very clearly that it is your Father as well as his Father. Therefore, if It was within him, It must be within us. What good is it to have a Father within, if we do not turn to It? Read the story of the Prodigal. He had a rich father, too, but he did not turn to his father; he turned to himself and ended up with the pigs.

Our entire faith, confidence, and hope must be in that Power which Paul called the "Christ [that] liveth in me."[2] Be assured, however, that merely saying that the "Christ liveth in me" will not bring It forth. You must contact It. Do not think that you can be in and of the world, and yet receive the divine Light flowing to you from within. But when you have made your contact with the Source, then, you can go about your business. As one approach to the making of that contact, try to meditate upon the reality of being. Then, turn within and rest; see what message comes to you from within. Never for a moment doubt but that you will receive an answer to your prayer or meditation. We look unto the hills, from whence cometh our help;[3] we look to the hills, or to the heights of consciousness. We look up, within our own being. We look up to the highest point of our own consciousness for help in every circumstance. We never look outside or beyond the limits of our own being.

Consciousness Forms the Body

God created all that was made.[4] That God is divine, infinite Consciousness, the consciousness of individual being. That Consciousness created your body, your home, your business. Everything of which you are aware is the emanation, expression, and manifestation of your consciousness, the Consciousness which is God.

Now what happens to us in the human picture? We "feed" the body which was created by divine Consciousness. We feed it from the outside, and because of our acceptance of the universal belief that the body is fed from without, we feel that it requires vitamins, calories, or something added to it from without. Do you remember when we were talking about supply, we came to the conclusion that supply, even in the form of money, must be as spiritual as the supply of truth itself? We also concluded that we could go within our own consciousness and find truth. Then we turn around and accept the belief that we must go outside for money! If it were true that there is a material universe, or, in other words, that there is a spiritual universe, plus a material universe, then it would follow that we could go within our own being for the spiritual things of life, but that we would have to go outside for the material things. That is not true.

The truth is that God is Spirit, and that God created this universe out of Its own being. All that God created is good. All that God created is spiritual substance and reality. Therefore, our body must be as spiritual as the consciousness of which it is formed. It must, therefore, be possible for our body to be fed from within, instead of from without.

If mortal sense tells us that we are underfed and undernourished, or that there is a deterioration of this piece of body or that piece of body—even a bone of the body—it must be possible to renew it through consciousness, which is the substance of our being, rather than by adding to the body from without. The only thing which prevents this from happening is our individual acceptance of a "matter I" and a "matter you," which results in our accepting as law the human belief that we are fed from without.

Everything in the teaching of the Infinite Way is an unfoldment, a statement or restatement of the teaching of the Master, Christ Jesus. When the disciples came to him and said, "Master, we have food for you," he answered, "I have meat to eat that ye know not of."[5]

What he meant was that he was being fed from within. Consciousness, Spirit, Life itself formed this thing that we call your body and my body. That Spirit, that Substance, is the meat that nourishes it. When we reverse the universal belief that we are being fed from without, that the food we are taking into our system is nourishing the body, and when we consciously accept the truth that we are fed from within, that the consciousness that formed the body is feeding and maintaining and sustaining it unto eternity, then we shall find the body is responding to spiritual law.

You may still go on eating, although of one thing I am certain: Your appetite will change; you will desire a different type of food, or less of certain foods. Why? Because no one can eat when he is filled, and you will be filled when you are drawing on spiritual food from within, twenty-four hours a day. We require the amount of food we do, because we are not being fed from within.

God, Spirit, divine Consciousness, is the causative principle of our body, as well as of our business, of our home, and of our social activities. God is the divine consciousness of our being, the substance of our being, and the law of our being; but we must turn within in order to start the flow that we, as human beings, have reversed.

Humanly, the body goes on for three score years and ten, but long before the three score years and ten are reached, it begins to deteriorate. The food from without does not do quite a complete job of feeding, sustaining, and renewing it. Therefore, even though we attempt to renew it by means of the food we eat, the body responds only seventy or eighty percent, continuing to waste away until it is ready for the grave. That will always be true in the human picture. Only you, individually, and I, individually, can reverse that picture, so that our body will function eternally, if we so desire it, and in the same state of perfection in which it was at the height of our youth and vitality. We determine that in this moment. We do it by consciously reversing the belief that the body is being fed and sustained from without by the food we eat and by accepting the spiritual truth that the same consciousness that formed the body is now feeding it, nourishing it, maintaining it, sustaining it, and renewing it unto eternity.

This must be a conscious process. It must become an activity of your consciousness, because consciousness is the creative principle of life. Immediately, the question arises, "Are you talking about the material body?" And the answer is that you do not have a material body. How could God create a material body? God is Spirit! God is consciousness! God is the creative principle of this universe! And God, the Infinite must create out of Its own Being. That which you have been calling a material body, treating as if it were a material body—feeding, clothing, and bathing—is your spiritual body. The only thing material about the body is our erroneous concept of it, and that erroneous concept did not begin with you or with me. It is a universal belief, a universal concept that we, individually, have accepted.

How could Jesus have walked through walls, or on the water? How could Peter have walked on the water? How could any of the miracles have been performed? And these miracles were not only performed by Jesus, but by many of the great prophets. Moses brought manna out of the sky and water out of a rock. How about Elijah and Elisha? What about Moses and the burning bush? How could there have been a burning bush that did not burn, if this were a material universe? In ignorance, we have accepted the universal belief, just as our ancestors accepted the belief that the world was flat. It was not flat. Yet the belief that the world was flat caused people to act as if it were and held them in bondage to a flat world just as if such a belief had been true.

The same sort of thing is operative with us. We are in bondage to the belief that we have a mortal, human, material body. That is why we are not walking through walls; but it is not for us to try to walk through walls. We can make higher demonstrations than that. To illustrate, there is a story concerning a Hindu who had been trying for many years to become spiritual. Finally, he came running to his master, saying elatedly, "Master, I have done a marvelous thing! I have walked all the way across the river on the water. And just think, it took me thirty years to accomplish it!"

The master's dry response was, "You could have crossed on the boat for two pennies." Such a feat was no miracle. In like manner, do not study for the purpose of learning how to walk through walls or on the water. No, there is something far more important that we should do. We should live to be ninety or one hundred years of age, looking as if we were twenty five. That is one thing we can do. But we will not do this by sitting around, hoping, or by looking at the person who has accomplished it, and saying, "I should love to be like that!"

The Body Is Maintained by Consciousness

You must begin to understand the law of creation. God is your individual consciousness and, therefore, it is your individual consciousness that is creating, feeding, nourishing, supporting, and maintaining your body in its health, harmony, and beauty unto all time, if you so desire it—unto all time, if you will but consciously realize that you are being fed, maintained, and sustained from within. If you do this, so will it be unto you.

You may be inclined to ask, "Is that important?" Yes, it is the most important part of your entire development. There is only one thing important in this world, and that is showing forth God as our life, as our substance, as our safety, our security, our immortality, our eternality, proving that God is the only law unto our being. If it is true that God is the only law unto our being, and that we are God-governed, God-maintained, and God-supported, then we should show it forth as youth, beauty, vitality, strength, intelligence, health, and all the other divine qualities. In other words, is there any virtue in preaching this truth, and then showing forth the opposite? There is none. None. Students have no right to go to the rest of the world and say, "You ought to study metaphysics; you ought to turn to God," and themselves show forth such a lack of awareness as to cause the world to retort, "Why?" By their fruits, you shall know them.

Ask yourself, "Am I showing forth the highest demonstration of which I am capable?" If not, is it not true that it is only because you are not sufficiently bringing this truth into conscious expression? In other words, are we not all sitting around believing there is a God somewhere, who is going to do something for us. "Let God do it!" In proportion to our lack of demonstration, do we indicate that we are not consciously bringing this into our experience, that we are not consciously renewing the body day by day. And we never will, so long as we think of nourishment as entering the body through the mouth. "Not that which goeth into the mouth defileth a man; but that which cometh out of the mouth."[6] It is not that which goes in that feeds us. It is that which comes out of the issues of the heart, the Soul, or consciousness, which is our food. Our demonstration is in proportion to our conscious awareness of the truth of being.

Health is not accidental. Harmony is not accidental. It may be out in the human world, where there are some human beings who are healthy all the time, or most of the time. Actually, though, such human beings are few and far between. Furthermore, we know nothing of what goes on in their consciousness to account for it, or what their pre-existent consciousness may have brought forth for them. This we know: If we want harmony, peace, jurisdiction, or dominion, we shall have to bring it into our experience through the conscious knowing of the truth. We must fulfill the words of the Master: "Know the truth, and the truth shall make you free."[7] We must not depend on the *truth* to make us free; we must depend on our conscious *awareness* of that truth.

We have embarked on a mission: the realization of God as divine consciousness unfolding as our individual being. We shall have to take the next step and realize that this body is maintained and sustained by the infinite Consciousness that formed it, the divine Consciousness of our being. We are eternally being fed, not three times a day, but twenty-four hours of every day, from within.

I have meat to eat that ye know not of.[8]
But whosoever drinketh of the water that I shall give him shall never thirst; but the water that I shall give him shall be in him a well of water springing up into everlasting life.[9] . . . the words that I speak unto you, they are spirit, and they are life.[10]

The Word—Consciousness—is life eternal. It is your consciousness. It is your consciousness as life eternal, since God is the universal consciousness of immortal being.

When we dispel the universal belief in the deterioration of organs, functions, or bone structure, we are renewed. Why? Because we do not have a physical body to be patched up, and the realization, that that consciousness which we are, constructed the body, functions as a renewal of the body. That consciousness will continue to keep the body in its original form, substance, youth, and beauty.

Spiritual Healing: The Mission of the Master

The ministry of the Master was spiritual healing. It did not make any difference whether it was a person with deformed bones, or a person whose organs had ceased to function in what we call death. His ministry was to restore consciousness, just as the Christ of your consciousness is present to restore even "the years of the locusts." That part of the body which already is dead or dying must be renewed by the Christ, by the state of consciousness which has been revealed to you as the substance of your being.

Let us go back to the beginning of this chapter to the statement that we never undertake anything without first going within, without that contact, that is, without meditation. If we truly expect that contact to come forth in the form of whatever is necessary for our demonstration, can it not come forth in the form of a body, organ, function, or bone? If it can come forth in the form of transportation or companionship or supply, why should it not come forth as body? It will come forth in every conceivable form necessary to the fulfilment of the Messianic mission, which is life eternal. The mission of the Master was to reveal life eternal to you and to me. Through what process? Through the process of a conscious awareness of truth, knowing the truth.

So must we, through that same Christ consciousness, renew and restore the organs and functions of our body. We can do that only in the degree that we realize that Consciousness, God, is the substance of our form, and that we are fed, nourished, supported, maintained, and sustained from within. That is true of our body; it is true of the substance of our business and of the substance of our home. We can be ever renewed, ever fresh, ever refilled with divine energy, if we knowingly contact the Source of our being, which is God, our individual consciousness.

Pay particular attention to these statements of the Master: "I have meat ye know not of. . . ."[11] The water that I shall give him shall be in him a well of water springing up into everlasting life."[12] This consciousness within your own being will spring up within you as eternal life—not eternal life after the body lies in the grave, but eternal life right here and now, conscious eternality, immortality, *in this form*. We are renewing the body now, day by day, in the understanding of the truth that God is Spirit, and that, therefore, the creative Principle is spiritual. That which is created is spiritually Self-supporting, Self-sustaining, and Self-maintaining. That is the eternal wellspring of water and the meat that the outer world knows nothing of.

In going within to meditate in order to touch that reality of our being, let us consciously realize that every time we touch this spring within, new life comes flowing forth. It makes the flesh vital, firm, and strong, because it is permeated with life from within. Consciousness does it, the Consciousness which is God.

Treatment as Silent Listening

When we are in the silence, that is a treatment. That is the type of treatment we give to every circumstance that arises in our experience. One by one, whether or not it is a problem of body, business, home relations, or some phase of health, we must hold to that type of treatment, not in the sense of a formula, not in the sense of making up a great many statements, but in the sense of letting the divine Consciousness tell us what the truth is.

A treatment must not consist of sitting down and going through a ritual of making statements about truth. A treatment must be a turning to the Father within, asking, "What is the truth about business, about body, about health, about my neighbor, about the universal belief of war?" and then letting the divine Consciousness tell it to you. Never believe that reading truth, memorizing it, or reciting it, will produce the effect you seek. These serve merely as a means to an end. You, yourself, must go within and let the divine Consciousness give you a treatment. You do not give the treatment. You receive the treatment from the Soul.

Is it clear, now, that everything has to come from within—even the treatment? A treatment is an impartation from within, and not lip service. Treatment is necessary so long as we are in ignorance, or so long as we are being handled by universal beliefs. In the degree that we are suffering from any form of sin, sickness, lack, or limitation, we need treatments, but not treatment from without. The treatment must be from within. Then you will find that that treatment is substance, is power, and is law.

Have you not wondered, sometimes, after you have remembered some of these made-up statements and faithfully repeated and repeated and repeated them, why you did not get the health, the harmony, or the wealth you expected from them? Those statements were external to you: You were stuffing sawdust into a doll; you were stuffing yourself with a made up "sawdust" treatment. Our treatment does not consist of made up thoughts; our treatment is a treatment of peace. It is a treatment of consciousness expressing itself. It comes entirely and directly out of meditation, and, in that degree, will it bring results. It will bear fruit in healings and improved health.

You must bring out the right sense of treatment, banish the idea of treatment by formula, and eliminate the idea that treatment can come out of books, or that you can use and repeat any treatment that is found in my writings or recordings. Treatment is powerful only when it comes through with all the power of God behind it. Treatment must come from the center within, from the divine consciousness of you. Then it is substance. Then it is feeding you, supporting you, maintaining you, and prospering you.

You do not give a treatment: You receive it, and you do not receive it from a man or a woman. You receive the treatment from God. God utters, voices, declares Itself from the center of your being to your conscious awareness. Then that treatment is a creative principle. If something comes through spiritually from God, it will renew you. You will be reborn, and you will die daily to the flesh. And by this I do not mean "passing on." I mean that you will lose mortality and gain immortality here and now. You will lose old age, and gain youth. You will lose decayed flesh, and find it renewed, if the treatment comes from within, if it has the substance of Truth, if it comes from out of consciousness to you.

Note to Active Workers

When a practitioner is very active in this practice, he may sometimes find that he does not feel well. Either he feels actual physical pain, distress, sickness, headaches, and the like, or he has depressed or discouraged feelings. All degrees of negative reactions may be experienced at different times. I do not mean that a practitioner suffers thus continuously, but he is likely to awaken either in the morning or at night with symptoms of disease or distress, or even to feel these in the middle of the day.

The first temptation is to ask, "What is wrong with me? This should not be happening to me." Let me caution workers about such a reaction. These symptoms are not really yours. They are caused by someone who is hammering at you for help, and you are not recognizing it. You are accepting the word "I," and taking all this in as if you yourself were sick. Be alert to this. Everyone who has been in this work knows that there are people reaching out to him, mentally, day and night—sometimes crying out to him. If you are not alert, you will take it personally and react to the negative emotion or feeling. If practitioners are not careful to hold up that word *I*, they may think of *I* as Jane, Jim, or Joel, not recognizing that when these negative things come to us, they indicate that others are reaching out for help.

To active workers, I say, please remember: First, keep that word *I* in its rightful place. Every time you think the word *I*, automatically know that you are thinking about God; second, realize, always, that the call for help is not to you—it is not a call to your human understanding. That call for help is to your developed state of consciousness, that state of consciousness which does the healing work. Those who are reaching out to it do not care about Jane, Jim, or Joel. All they care about is to reach that developed state of consciousness which is a healing consciousness. They do not care from whom or through whom the healing comes.

If we had the ability, we could turn back to Jesus Christ, to the mind that was in Christ Jesus and through that find healing. We do not do so only because we perhaps think that the interval of years separates us from that mind, not realizing that the mind of Christ Jesus is here and is our mind.

Active workers, whether you are healing, teaching, lecturing, or writing, please remember that somebody, somewhere, is reaching out to you. As that someone touches your human mentality, you may feel a drag on you. What some might call transference of thought may even occur, so that you believe that you are sick, whereas it is the person calling out, telling you that he is in need of help. At the very first sign of illness, discouragement, or fear, be alert and realize that someone is reaching out to the Christ, not to any human identity or mentality. He is seeking the Christ of his own being, and that Christ is responding. Know: "This suggestion of malpractice cannot use my mind for its operation or outlet." Be alert to these conditions. Never must a practitioner identify his personal selfhood with the practice. It is the Christ that is the practitioner, and it is the Christ that is handling the practice. It is not a person. Practitioners will be dragged down if they let themselves be drawn upon as human beings, or if they do not recognize that these negative things coming to them are only the pull of patients and the pull of the world on them.

Instead of looking at the human world and trying to change it, sit back and get at-one with Spirit; try to catch the vision of what the spiritual universe or spiritual activity is. In other words, do not try to think of the person who has the cold, or try to help him to get rid of it. Inasmuch as the cold has no reality, there is no use trying to get rid of it. But so long as it presents itself as an appearance, certainly something must be done about it. That something is to get at-one with the Infinite, with Spirit, with Soul, and watch reality unfolding—watch the real truth, the real being, come to light. The idea is to stop fighting this world picture; stop fighting the Adam-dream; stop fighting illusion. Sit down and get at peace, and let the reality unfold and disclose itself.

~5~

FREEDOM IN CHRIST

It is a very difficult thing to impart the idea of Christ wisdom. Christ wisdom differs from human knowledge, even from a human knowledge of truth. Humanly, none of us knows what truth is. Certainly no one knows with the human mind what it is. The wisdom of Christ is not in the realm of human wisdom or understanding. It is a knowledge that transcends all earthly wisdom. The things of God are foolishness with men.[1] In the moment when we recognize that we know nothing about this, and we are not just being modest, in the moment when we go to the Father and humbly say, "I don't know what this is all about, Father," in that moment we begin to touch the hem of the garment.

We talk about truth, and we write about truth. We never voice *Truth. Only God voices Itself.* Only Wisdom, Itself, voices Itself to us, and sometimes through us. In actual truth, It is voicing Itself as us: *"I* am the truth . . . *I* am the life. . . . *I* am the infinite wisdom of the universe." That, in its spiritual meaning, is absolute truth, but that *I* is not a man, woman, or child; it is not the human "I". That *I* is God. And when It voices Itself, the wisdom of the ages becomes known. The power of Spirit and Soul becomes visible and tangible, and we see the dead rise; we see the sick and sinning healed; we see some body "lighting up" with a look of wisdom beyond anything of this earthly realm.

"Though I speak with the tongues of men and of angels,"[2] if I do not have that divine love which takes no cognizance of mortals and mortal experience, it is not God talking. The entire trouble with our demonstration is the word "I." It is not that we would not subdue the "I," not because we cling to it so much, not because we would not gladly do away with that little "I" or ego; it is not that we would not say, "Not my will, but thine, be done." It is the universal belief of a selfhood apart from God that so forces itself into our thought that we, even we who set ourselves up as having attained a measure of spirituality, sometimes say, "I have wisdom," or, "I know the truth," or, "I know God." That is never true. It is only true when that little "I" is not there. It is only true when God is declaring Itself, as It did through Jesus, as It did after Jesus, and as It has done through the lips of many wise men and women down through the ages.

When we begin to understand, even in a slight measure, that what we know with the human mind is not spiritual wisdom, we are then beginning to understand the next step which is our freedom in Christ, our freedom in God. You and I cannot experience freedom of our own. We cannot experience health of our own, nor can we experience wealth of our own. It is only in the degree that we experience God, and the freedom of God made manifest as our experience, that we can understand the immortality of God made manifest as our individual being. Only as we are able to recognize Christ as being always like a cloud around us in Its freedom and Its tenderness, do we begin to understand what it means to be able to say, "I have no freedom, no health, no wealth of my own. It is the will of God, the life of God, made manifest as me. The life of God is immortal and eternal. It is health, wealth, harmony, wholeness, peace, joy, and dominion. It is all things of a spiritual nature."

We fail because, with the intellect, we try to bring God down to human terms; we try to connect God with a human being. We think of it as the life of God "in me," and thereby, set up a "me" separate from the life of God. We think we have or can attain the wisdom of God, but only God has the wisdom of God. As we begin to understand that, this little "me" folds up and disappears. Then wisdom comes through, in and of itself.

In the awareness that God, infinite Being, is the only reality of being, and that God alone has the wisdom of God, we are beginning to touch the hem of the Robe. Let us not claim anything for ourselves; let us not even claim understanding. Let us realize that God is the only understanding, the only One who understands, and that God is the manifestation of Its own understanding, since God is all-in-all.

God is life. Does that leave room for any other life? Do we have to connect the life which is God with Jones or Brown or Smith? Isn't it enough to know that God is the one and only life?

God is wisdom. Do we have to connect it with a person? Is it not enough that God is infinite wisdom? As long as God is infinite wisdom, there can be no other wisdom, nor can there be any lack of a wisdom which is infinite. Let us be careful to let God be wise. We might go another step and let God be the all-wise, the only wisdom. And you know that would include us, since the infinity of God cannot leave us out.

The freedom of our being is really a freedom in Christ. Freedom is wholeness, completeness, and harmony. Let us, therefore, understand the freedom of Christ. Then we shall understand and begin to feel some measure of the freedom of our own being. Do not be satisfied with less than the unfoldment of truth from your highest standpoint.

Treatment: An Impartation of Divine Ideas

In the unfoldment in this book, we have said much about treatment that we have not said before. We have taken up the subject of treatment from a higher standpoint. Treatment, as it has been revealed here, is the divine idea on any particular subject, unfolding and disclosing itself to us, and this divine idea should be revealed in its completeness, so that when we sit down and ask for a treatment on business, all that is to be known on the subject of business should disclose and reveal itself within our own being. We do not ask a person for a treatment on business, even when we go to a practitioner. At that moment, we are turning to the one mind, healing as a practitioner.

Ultimately, that one mind will appear. as our own consciousness, and we shall receive the treatment from within our own being. We have the right to go within for treatment on any subject and, ourselves receive the treatment from God. Let the voice of God utter Itself to us from within and reveal Itself to us in Its fullness on any subject. Let us learn to discard any other method of treatment and begin to understand treatment as something that we receive as unfoldment and revelation on health, body, business, or relationships in our daily affairs. Let us begin to understand that we, ourselves, may receive enlightenment on any given subject from within our own being.

I have said over and over again that prayer is not a petitioning of God. Prayer is the word of God which we receive in silence. Now we are lifting treatment up a step higher. Treatment, now, will not be a knowing of the truth from without. It will be a knowing of the truth from within. It will be a divine realization of the truth of being as it pertains to any subject on which we require or want enlightenment.

Harmony through Christ is the release from the belief of mortal selfhood. It is not the relief of disordered organs or functions of the body. Harmony, through Christ, is the ascent into the realization of our Christ identity. We have a Christ identity, and it is more real than our human identity. Of the human identity, Jesus said, "I have power to lay it down, and I have power to take it again."[3] And that is true of our human identity. Anything can happen today or tomorrow to this human identity. But our spiritual identity in Christ is permanent and eternal. Because this is so, that which appears to you as the human "me," and that which appears to me as the human "you," actually, is an immortal and eternal being here on earth.

We, on this path, will not die. No evidence to the contrary will ever convince us that we can die, or that we can age, or that we can fail. It cannot be. We have taken upon ourselves the identity of Christ in which is freedom. Remember not to use the word Christ just because you have read it in Scripture, or in metaphysical literature. Use it because Christ is a reality. Christ is something so vital, so real, that we cannot demonstrate It unless we understand it. Life in Christ means freedom from bondage to the organs and functions of the body. Harmony in Christ means freedom from the belief of bondage to dollars and cents. Harmony in Christ means freedom from inharmonious human relationships, whether they be family, business, national, or international. When we have put on Christ, mortality will have disappeared. When we have put on our Christ identity and have stopped relating ourselves to human birth, maturity, and ultimately death, we shall have achieved immortality here and now.

Time and Space

Immortality has nothing to do with time, even though that is how we think of it. Time has nothing to do with Truth. You can collapse all time into this second; the moment you can rise above the limitations of human finiteness, you can see past, present, and future simultaneously. It has been done over and over again, even from the human standpoint. We can have limitless vision from the human standpoint, if we broaden consciousness. It is not true that the eyes see only that which is within eyesight, and the ears hear only that which is within earshot. There is no limit when consciousness is not so bounded. It all depends upon the activity of consciousness. As long as we identify ourselves with physicality, we are limited to the body. But the very moment we can find our freedom in Christ, we have no such limitation.

I do not leave my body. Do not believe that you can leave the body. That is just a seeming, a sense that comes to us to show us the limitless nature of our Christ-Self. And this will come at a time and in a place in which we can show forth some lesson or some proof of unlimited time and space. If you want to understand reincarnation, pre-existence, and immortality, separate them from the belief of time. Try to think of what the past means when the past is happening now. Try to think of what the future means when the future is taking place now. When you can see past, present, and future, all in one moment, then you will understand these subjects.

Reincarnation, pre-existence, immortality—these three subjects mean Consciousness unfolding, Consciousness revealing Itself at the standpoint of our particular understanding. There is no such thing as a physical universe. If there were a physical universe, time and space would be real. There is no way yet to prove that time and space are not real, although physicists have proved it to their own satisfaction and will prove it to ours before the end of time. Meanwhile, in order to avoid the limitations of time and space, close your eyes and watch your consciousness unfold and disclose itself, and see how unlimited consciousness is.

Now that we have come to the place where we see that we are living a life, not in time and space, but as consciousness, then are not health and wealth a matter of consciousness? Are they not the unfoldment of our own consciousness in the *form* of health and wealth? Must not consciousness always have a form? If consciousness did not have form, it would be non-existent. The moment consciousness has existence, it has existence as something, and that something must be as forms of reality. The reality of being, whether of mind, body, or purse, is Consciousness unfolding Itself individually, on the level of our receptivity here and now.

Health is not a condition of body, but a condition of consciousness. Wealth is not a condition of purse, but of consciousness. When you learn to close your eyes and think in terms of consciousness, "I am consciousness," then the question comes, "As consciousness, what am I conscious of expressing?" All that will come to you is that you are conscious of consciousness itself in its infinite form and variety. Consciousness is God; therefore, all that you can be conscious of is God appearing to you as a person, a place, or a thing. And that brings us back to the statement that God is all-in-all.

That statement, however, is really too simple. We have to make it a little more difficult, in order to understand the simplicity of it. The statement of itself is very nearly meaningless until we understand the following points:

1. God is consciousness.
2. God is the consciousness which I am.
3. The consciousness which I am must reveal itself to me in the form of my ability to understand and utilize.

Then we come back to Consciousness unfolding, disclosing, revealing, manifesting, and expressing Itself as our individual being and as all that concerns us.

Freedom in Christ means freedom in Consciousness, the understanding of the Consciousness that is God, and the freedom of that infinite Consciousness. And when we understand that "I am that Consciousness," then we understand that we are not limited by physical boundaries, not even those of time and space. It is not enough to realize that we are not bound by the limitations of the body. We must overcome the belief of the limitation of time and space. Then we begin to understand immortality and eternality. Otherwise, immortality means only longevity, and eternality but permanence.

That is why, in spiritualism, we have the belief that the life, which in reality we are, has left its embodiment but continues on in its same intelligence and wisdom. It is true that the life which we are never dies, that it is not limited to body, to material sense, and that, therefore, it certainly cannot be limited to a grave. However, this is not carrying the subject far enough. We must unfold and reveal the final step: The body is forever as infinite, as eternal and immortal, as life itself, for life and body are one. Life and body are inseparable. Jesus did not die and then return. Jesus proved the immortality of his life and the immortality of the body. He returned in the same body.

We do not demonstrate immortality, so long as we find it necessary to experience death, or "passing on," in order to continue the life of the Soul. We must ourselves determine the experience. We determine health through the realization of the body's being as immortal as the mind, or as life, itself. Even when you begin to understand life as immortal, you will not improve the health of your body until, and unless, you see the body as a formation of the consciousness of your own being. When you begin to see that, as consciousness, you are appearing here in manifested form, then you have made yourself immortal—not through death, but through living. That is freedom in Christ. It is freedom from the belief in mortality. When you have put off mortality and put on immortality here and now, the body will show forth youth, strength, vitality, health, harmony, and wholeness.

Do not separate mind and body; do not separate consciousness and body; do not divide yourself in any way. Do not separate any part of your experience from consciousness. Learn to close your eyes and begin to realize your life as consciousness. Then, when you have realized your life as consciousness, you will have found your freedom in Christ. The body will then be what it was intended to be: a form in which to appear, a form to use. Then we shall come into the experience of a body without pain, without deterioration, without age, and without change.

We are demonstrating this and proving it in a measure—but only in a measure. We have seen some of our people in the metaphysical world who have had wonderful demonstrations of this harmony of being and harmony of body. That we have not gone further is due only to the fact that we are not realizing fully our existence as consciousness. We are still believing in a beginning and in an ending. We are believing in time and space.

You will not demonstrate youth and health, strength and vitality of body until you learn to transcend this belief of time and space. That can come only as you see yourself as consciousness, as a state of awareness, and then say: "How could that have beginning, and how can that end? How can you bind that up in a body or a grave?" With that beginning, with that realization, comes your freedom in Christ.

I emphasize this phrase, "freedom in Christ," or "freedom in spiritual identity," because there is no other freedom. If you try to gain freedom for your mind, your person, or your purse, you will fail. If you realize your freedom as a state of consciousness, you will succeed, and you will not have to particularize it by saying, "That applies to my heart, or my head." You will be content to experience your freedom in Christ, and let it translate itself into terms of that which we call human good. There is a freedom in the state of consciousness that realizes that it, itself, is infinite, and that it has transcended all time, place, and space. When that freedom is felt, it is felt by all those who come into the atmosphere of that consciousness. That is what was happening in Jesus' consciousness when he healed the multitudes that thronged around him. It was the freedom he had in his own consciousness that became the freedom of his patients.

The freedom that you attain in your consciousness is the degree of freedom that will be attained by those who seek help from you. You cannot take the "I" of a human being and lift it up into spiritual freedom. That is what has been hampering us, and that is what we are going to break, so that we will attain this freedom in Christ. How? By realizing that the *I* is God, not a person. Let us learn that, here and now. There is an "I" calling itself a person, and it would love to lift itself up and say, "I am spiritual." That "I" is not spiritual at all. God is Spirit; God is the life, the substance, and the reality of all being and of all form. God is the freedom of Its creation; God is the substance, law, and reality of Its creation. Let us realize that God is the freedom of all being, the mind and the Soul and the law of, and unto, its own creation. In God, in Christ, is freedom from the personal sense of "I."

The Spiritual Plan

We have said that there is a spiritual, universal plan. Since God is infinite intelligence, God must operate or act as an infinite plan of good for Its universe. Just as we plan our business and the details of our existence, so must infinite Intelligence in Its spiritual way, bring everything into one divine pattern, nothing out of place and no one out of place, but everything and everyone fulfilling the spiritual function that they were created to perform. We, in our limited understanding, have no awareness of what the spiritual plan is. But there is a spiritual universe, and we are spiritual beings, and as such, we are part of the spiritual plan. We are fulfilling that function as human beings. It was never intended that we be either rich or poor, successful or unsuccessful, sick or well. We are functions, activities, and capacities of the divine spiritual Consciousness. As such we are part of a universal whole, and each one of us is working for the good of the whole in our spiritual identity. Humanly, we do not know what that plan is. We have strayed away from the Father's house, from our spiritual identity, until we have become lost.

Now, through meditation, we are turning to the inner Consciousness, asking for light: "What is the plan, Father, for the spiritual universe, and what is my part in that plan?" We have the right to know, if necessary, the whole of the plan, since we are the manifested activity of the entire spiritual realm, infinite and immortal. We can see and know the entire spiritual realm, infinite and immortal. We can see and know the entire plan; we can and we must, ultimately, know where we fit into the spiritual picture.

I have said before that the function of this work is not that we should be a little healthier or a little wealthier. The purpose of this work is the revealing of God as our individual consciousness, so that we may fit ourselves into that ultimate plan and learn what our destiny is, even here on earth. Do you think there is only a human existence on earth? No, this human picture is not God's plan for you. There is another answer, and that answer will be brought forth by those of us who in meditation touch the hem of the Robe, touch the center of the Eternal, bringing down to human consciousness an answer to all of the problems we are facing today.

Never forget this: The world, as a human world, is not the real world. There is nothing that we should or can do about the human situation. It is all a question of unfoldment. There must be a transcendental working out of all errors. To do that, we turn to God and realize the presence of God in operation at all times and in all places. We are to lift thought up out of its material sense and bring to light a spiritual awakening. The metaphysician does not remove a growth or an obstruction; but through spiritual realization, some great spiritual activity is set up in consciousness, and it dissolves this seeming error.

No Unsolvable Problems

This same principle should be applied to world conditions and world affairs. Errors are real only to the mortal sense of reality. They are not real in the spiritual realm, and they are not real to the student of spiritual reality. There is no solution to them, except as someone, somewhere, touches the divine Consciousness and brings truth to light. If you and I can touch infinity every day of the week, and if, when confronted by these world problems, we can realize: "Father, there is a divine plan, but it does not lie in the realm of my human thinking, or in the realm of any human thinking.

There is a spiritual universe, just as there is a spiritual body, which I bring forth through spiritual enlightenment; and, therefore, there is a spiritual solution to every problem on earth."

Most of the cases that come to us come only after the doctor says that there is no hope. The metaphysical movement is made up of the living "dead," those whom the doctors had pronounced near death, years and years ago, but who are still walking the earth. They are the living proof that neither life nor its individual formation can be destroyed. They are the living proof that for every condition the world calls sin, disease, or death, there is a spiritual light, a spiritual consciousness, which will dispel it. Is there any difference between the healing of such conditions and the healing of what the world calls an international debt, or an unsolvable international problem? No. We have the solution for every problem ever existing and sufficient spiritual enlightenment to reveal it. That is all that is required—enlightened consciousness.

The light of God must shine through as individual consciousness. That spiritual light appears as a man or a woman. It appears in a language we can understand. Deep as are the problems of the world today, unsolvable as they seem to be under human thinking and human planning, in reality, there is no such thing as an unsolvable problem. But the solution will be revealed only by those who turn within to the kingdom of God and touch that lighted center of their own being. These will bring forth the light, and to the world, such a one may appear as another Jesus of Galilee or another Saul of Tarsus. Someone will come to light at the necessary moment and it may not be one, but a dozen.

The Spiritual Universe

God is Spirit, and the world of God's creation is spiritual. We have proved that our body is spiritual by the fact that in turning to Spirit, we have brought about the harmony of our body, which we have termed health or healing. We have proved that supply is spiritual, because by applying spiritual consciousness to the subject of business or supply, we have brought about either a greater sense of business or supply, or a more harmonious sense. Everyone in the metaphysical world has proved in some degree that what appears as a material universe is subject to spiritual treatment. If this has done nothing else, it has proved that this is a spiritual, and not a material universe.

All these so-called problems in the world can and must be solved by bringing to light the reality of spiritual jurisdiction over the universe of God's creation. This we must each do for our individual selves. We must go into meditation. We must stay in meditation until we feel a response which says, *"I* am here. The presence of God is here, 'Lo, *I* am with you alway, even unto the end of the world.' "[4] And we must do this same thing for the world. Remember that your private life is not something separate and apart from the rest of the world. Your private life is as much a part of the world as all of us are part of each other.

You have only to understand this, and you will find that your relationship with every individual in the world, regardless of country, race, creed, or color, is the same. There is an invisible bond between every individual on earth. This bond is a spiritual bond. Never believe for a moment that I, in my meditation, have not touched it. It was that which gave birth to the statement: "My oneness with God constitutes my oneness with all spiritual being and idea." My oneness with God—never doubt this! There is an invisible bond between all the people of the world. We are all brothers, sisters, uncles, and cousins, not in a human sense, but in a spiritual sense. We cannot go out into the world humanly and be a brother or a sister to all the world, but we can sit down in our meditation and touch that center of God-being. We find, in doing that, that we have touched the life of every other being. We are all one in Christ.

We have no right to think that we are here for the purpose of squeezing a little bit of health or wealth out of God for ourselves. That is too selfish a purpose, and it will not work, because the vision is not on that level. It is on the level of God and the spiritual universe, and of trying to determine: "What is this principle of living? What is God? What is the spiritual universe?" Patching up a material universe, or using truth merely for a selfish purpose is not enough for us in our state of development. In the degree, however, that we turn to God and receive illumination, our own individual affairs will show forth the measure of our enlightenment. It would be folly to say, "I have touched God and I have overcome the world, but I have neither health nor wealth of my own." You can be sure that anyone who says that has not touched the kingdom of God within. There must be some degree of demonstration in your individual experience and in mine in order that we may show forth this experience to the rest of the world. You cannot fail to show forth better health and wealth, you cannot fail to show forth a more pleasant face or a happier experience to the world if you touch the hem of the Robe in your meditation. The minute you do touch that hem, you become a shining light and an example to the rest of the world. But even that is not enough.

There is a spiritual universe, a spiritual plan, which you will discern within your inner being. It is something that is not a part of the physical universe. Yet, when you touch it, it makes what appears as a physical universe look healthier or happier. Try taking the world into your meditation. Take in the entire world and think of it as trying to make contact with God. Through your contact with God, look out over the whole universe. See what it looks like from a spiritual standpoint. Find the center of your being and touch your inner consciousness—know God—and then look out on the spiritual horizon and see what the spiritual plan is: "Father, let me see this spiritual universe and the spiritual plan, and my part in it."

When you turn within in meditation, asking the Father to show you the spiritual universe, you will see trees from which the leaves never fall, trees on which the fruit is always in season. The trees in the spiritual universe are never bare, and there are no seasons of barrenness in between. You will find a universe in which the sun is always shining, and where it never sets, leaving a place of darkness. That is the spiritual universe. It is as Jesus described it when he said: "Say not ye, There are yet four months, and then cometh harvest? behold, I say, unto you, Lift up your eyes, and look on the fields; for they are white already to harvest."[5] You will find nothing in this spiritual universe that is offensive, or that must be reformed, and, furthermore, you will find no deterioration. You will see the Son of God coming with light.

Meditation as Consciousness Unfolding

My attention was first drawn to meditation through the life of Jesus, through the discovery of a higher sense of prayer, through trying to touch Consciousness, and through learning that conscious awareness was always attained through listening and receiving. You will remember Jesus said: "I can of mine own self do nothing[6] . . . the Father that dwelleth in me, he doeth the works."[7] He was always receiving from within through meditation.

As I pursued my study of the religions and philosophies of the world, I learned that this was the secret of every saint and of every person who had ever touched the hem of the Robe. It was the secret of Buddha, Shankara, Lao-Tse, Paul, Peter, John, of all the Catholic saints, the Hebrew prophets, and the Protestant brothers. With all of them, there was an ability to discern something inwardly. We call it meditation. I learned early in my own work that there was a secret that I could not find in all my study and reading. Then I learned to close my eyes, get at peace within, and perhaps in that moment, or a day or two later, the answer would come.

So began my own meditation. I was in this work less than two years when I discovered that the only results I had came through meditation. They came through sitting down, getting quiet, becoming receptive, and listening. Then, with a sudden rush, this feeling, this sense of the Presence would come, and the healings would take place. Or it would give me enlightenment: I would open a book at the right place; I would be led to a book, and find the right answer there. All of this came through the inward touching of something, until I made the discovery that there is a spiritual universe, a "temple not made with hands, eternal in the heavens," and that it can be discerned on this plane of existence, but not with the human mind.

The healing Presence comes into operation only when the human mind is not at work, when the mind is still and the senses are silent. When are the senses silent? Only in meditation, when we are at peace, when we dwell in an inner silence. It was then that I found the entire secret of life. There is nothing unknown to the person who meditates. There is nothing that can ever remain a secret—whether on the human or on the spiritual plane. Nobody can hide from me any truth I need to know, any unseen fact that I need to know. Everything I need to know comes to my experience, just when I need to know it. Why? Because having made the contact within, It brings all there is into outer manifestation. But this has nothing at all to do with the human mind.

"The kingdom of God is within you."[8] Then where are you going to find the kingdom of God? Not outside, certainly! Not in the activity of the human plane! As a matter of fact, all of our problems come from the activity of the human mind. When the human mind is still, the solution to those problems comes forth. The Christ consciousness is your individual expression of the universal God consciousness. It is God individually expressed by you or by me. It is the mind that was in Christ Jesus. The mind of God was the mind of Christ Jesus when it was individualized as the man Jesus.

Let us realize this: There is a God, an infinite Spirit, and there is a spiritual universe. But we know so little about either God or the spiritual universe, and we know so little about our particular place in that universe. So let us devote at least one of our meditation periods each day to the purpose of going within and finding the answer, within our own being, to the questions: What is God? What is the spiritual universe? What is the spiritual plan, and what is my part in it?

~6~

LIFTING OF CONSCIOUSNESS

The knowledge of the letter of this message, alone, is valueless. The real value lies in spiritual realization, accompanied by healing. "By their fruits ye shall know them."[1] To be able to memorize and talk about the Infinite Way, and yet not to be able to perform a reasonable degree of healing work, serves little purpose. There is already too much writing and printing of books, and, according to Scripture, too much talking about truth. Those who carry on this work must be those who have some measure of realization, who are not afraid when called upon to give help, and who can bring out healings.

The world does not need any more teaching: It does need more healing. Ours is, and will continue to be, a healing ministry, as long as those who are carrying on this ministry have caught enough realization of truth to do healing work. Some day people may read the Infinite Way books, and talk or preach about them, and then reply, when asked about healing, "Oh, that happened in Joel Goldsmith's own time, when he was still around." That is what we want to avoid. We want each one to catch the spiritual vision, and to go forth and do likewise.

There is enough spiritual reading in your Bible so that no words of mine are necessary. The Gospel according to John is enough. No other book is really necessary. If you could catch the spiritual vision of that book, you would need no metaphysical books. It is the most spiritual writing known to man. There is enough truth in it for all the healing ministries that will ever be called forth by human need. But the writings of today, because they are in our language and of our day, clarify those older writings. For that reason, our study and practice are made easier if we utilize the more recent interpretations.

When I say that only those should become active in this work, who are willing to be called upon for healing, I mean that we want to be doers; we do not want simply another generation of preachers. No person should push the doing of healing work off on to another fellow. Each student should accept the responsibility for healing. Healing is not a private or secret ministry. The healing work is not reserved for practitioners. Healing is for anyone and everyone—"greater works than these shall he do."[2] Anyone who devotes himself to this teaching receives a spiritual answer from within. He soon finds that the greatest development of healing power comes when he is asked for help and quickly says, "Yes!" without stopping to think. Why? Because that indicates his realization that it is not the human being or the human understanding that heals, but that it is the *I,* the spiritual identity, which can and will do the work.

The minute you say that you have not been reading or studying long enough to heal, you are admitting or claiming that a human being can heal. As a human being, of course, you cannot heal, even though you could recite from memory all the books ever written on the subject of healing. But when you are called upon for help, and you respond quickly with, "Certainly!" that is your recognition that error is nothingness and that you do not have to heal it.

What is the whole secret of the healing work? Is it that we have a power over error? Or is it that disease is not a power? This is not a teaching which says that by some kind of a miracle given to us we are able to overcome sin, disease, and death. It is a teaching which recognizes no reality in sin, disease, and death. These are illusions which have fooled us into believing them real. We have allowed ourselves to become frightened unto death by germs, infection, and contagion, even though we have had seventy or more years of metaphysical practice to prove that there is no truth or power in such things. Our practitioners go into homes where all of these are rampant, and rarely, very rarely, have they taken on the disease.

Ours is not a teaching of a secret way to overcome a great power called "error." Ours is a realization of its nothingness! That is how frightened we are of disease! When someone asks you for help, do not be afraid to say, "Certainly! I will give you help." The only understanding required for such a response is the understanding of the unreality of what appears as sin, disease, death, lack, or limitation.

Turn Ye, and Live

We are going to revise our entire concept of the purpose of our study and our life in truth. We are not to use our understanding of truth to make the human picture conform to our idea of what it should be. We are not to look at a person and decide that he should be healthier or wealthier, that he should or should not be employed. When a problem is brought to us, our mode or method of working is not to try to make a demonstration according to the way the patient thinks it should be made, which, by the way, sometimes does happen to the very great sorrow and regret of the patient.

We are not to judge from appearances. We are to "judge righteous judgement."[3] So, if we look out into the human world and see war threatening, it is not a part of our work to sit down and do some praying that no war take place. "Whatsoever a man soweth, that shall he also reap."[4] In Oriental Scripture, this is called the law of karma. It means that what you do today, that is, your conduct and thoughts of today, will result in a certain state of affairs tomorrow. In philosophy, this is called cause and effect. In the old Hebrew Scripture, it is given thus: "They that plow iniquity, and sow wickedness, reap the same."[5]

Think now of a roomful of people, meeting and consecrating themselves to truth, to love, and to peace. Then think for a moment, if you can, of conflict—a war—among them. Would it be possible for hate, envy, or fear to make progress in a room where people were gathered together in "*My* name?" No, it would not! There is too much love, too much of the Christ, too much peace in the hearts and Soul and consciousness of such people for conflict to be anything but impossible and unthinkable.

Now then, let us reverse the picture. Let us suppose wrangling goes on, and one person wants the job of another, someone else the money of another, while yet another is scheming for the social position of someone else. Tell me, if I were a witness to that, what kind of a prayer would I have to pray to save them from their own folly? Is there any prayer that could do it? So it is with the affairs of the world. "Whatsoever a man soweth, that shall he also reap."[6]

But there is a way to wipe out even this law of Jesus, the law of "as ye sow." That way is to "turn ye even to me with all your heart."[7] That way is to rebuild. That way is to have a change of consciousness. It does not make any difference what kind of sinner you were a month ago, what sins of omission or of commission you were guilty of, since you have dropped all that and you are now letting only peace and love and the divine Consciousness be active. Your past is wiped out, and there are no consequences from anything in your past. "Turn . . . and live."[8] Rebuild!

In the same way, if whole nations of people were to say, "We have been doing the wrong thing. We must stop all this trickery and get down to honest, fair, and just actions"; then all their past sins would be wiped out. They would have overcome all the sins of which they had ever been guilty. They would have overcome the old pattern, and their lives would be lived in accordance with their change of heart. They would receive the effect, then, of the new cause they have set in motion, which is reformation, and the old would truly be wiped out.

So our work, then, is not to sit down and say prayers that no war will come. In the first place, those prayers are voiced in the belief that what is happening in the human universe is reality, and it is not. It is illusion, whether the appearance be war or peace. It is the same as seeing one human being with a healthy body, and another with a sick body. In both cases, it is illusion.

Treatment Is Self-Treatment

Our object is to become one with the law of God, recognizing not even a healthy physical body, but only a purely spiritual body. Whereas, heretofore, if a person telephoned and said, "I have a headache," or "I am sick," we sat down immediately to do some work to correct that, now, in this new consciousness in which we are functioning, we do not do that at all. Now, we merely sit down to feel the conscious presence of God, to commune with the Infinite, and then let the spiritual harmony come forth. So you see that in this new and modern method of treatment, actually, the practitioner gives the practitioner the treatment about the patient.

A practitioner says, "Wait a minute! What kind of a suggestion is this that is coming to me of a selfhood apart from God, of a human being in pain, in sin, or in disease? I cannot accept that. I will not allow the imposition of such a belief on my consciousness. I will not allow my mind to be handled by such a belief. I know the truth that God is the reality, the substance, and the law of all being." The practitioner gives himself a treatment until he, himself, can say, "I am convinced!" The practitioner has not reached out and touched the patient's thought. But because of oneness, the patient feels that treatment. He feels the truth coursing through him, the truth in the practitioner's consciousness. He feels Truth, Itself, touching his consciousness, and he responds to It.

When I look out at you with my eyes I am not seeing *you;* I am seeing my concept of you and the universal concept of you; I am seeing a finite sense or concept of you. For me to try to patch that up, would be like taking a photograph of you and daubing on a little paint here

~112~

and there. It might improve the photograph, but it would never touch or change you. No matter how much we talk about this concept of you, it would still have nothing to do with *you*, because you are invisible to human sight. You are hidden behind your eyes, and no one can see you. The only thing about you that can be seen is whatever concept the world has built up regarding you, and that is not you. You are spiritual consciousness, and you have never been seen. You cannot be seen or touched. You are pure consciousness.

But you can be discerned in enlightened spiritual moments, in that sanctuary which is the temple of God, which I am. There, I am face to face with God, and I can know you as you are. That results in healing, a healing through spiritual discernment, but never through the five physical senses.

There is no use in declaring, "There is no war, depression, or accident," in an attempt to avert these disasters, or in the vain hope of eliminating them. Our effort is on the side of attaining a conscious oneness with God and letting this realization carry us through whatever war, depression or accident may appear in the world of illusion. It is possible, where we become one with God consciousness, where we are in tune with this infinite Power, for the whole of the presence and power of God to descend upon a community or a nation in its entirety and to eliminate some or all of the erroneous conditions.

Agree with Your Adversary

Do not, however, let your thought go out in an attempt to heal the world. That would only be an attempt to change the dream-picture, since war, depression, and accidents are not realities. Do not use your mind or your thought or your spiritual powers trying to patch up the illusion. Become one with God—and stay on that level of consciousness. Do this as many times as you can in the day, and as many times as you can during the night. Get the feeling of God's presence. Soon the illusion will be dispelled. Let this understanding reveal the illusory nature of that which appears as war, depression, or accident. Stop looking at the illusion and trying mentally to juggle it out of existence! Learn the meaning of "Agree with thine adversary."[9] To agree with your adversary means not to fight or try to change the mortal picture. It means to understand immediately that it is not a reality. That is your agreement.

Jesus did not deny crucifixion, nor did he audibly assert, "I am not afraid of Pilate." He did not "handle the error" of crucifixion, or "affirm freedom." He turned from both crucifixion and freedom, and declared God to be the only power acting in the consciousness of man, even of Pilate. "Thou couldest have no power at all against me, except it were given thee from above."[10]

Jesus did not ask God to "protect" him from Pilate's power. He did not say that Pilate had no power. He agreed that Pilate had power, but it was the power that was given him by God. Do you see the difference? We have here a new and higher concept of treatment and of living. Jesus did not deny that Judas would betray him. He proved, rather, that betrayal was not a power or a reality. He did not deny lack or limitation when he had only a few loaves and fishes with which to feed five thousand. He lifted his consciousness above that scene and realized God's presence, the presence of Allness, and It fed the multitudes. Jesus looked up and thanked the Father for that which is the presence of God. Since God is infinite being, he was thanking God for the infinity of loaves and fishes.

Never use your understanding to change, alter, correct, improve, or heal the human scene. Lift your consciousness. Look up to the Father above the human scene. Realize God's allness and then witness that Allness as fulfilment. How do we realize Allness? The moment you lift your thought to God, you have lifted it to Infinity. There is no such thing as limitations once you lift your thought to Consciousness which is God. Neither is there matter, nor sin, nor disease, nor discord. Only in the degree that you can look up and behold the face of God, can you see that all that emanates from God is good—eternal life, immortal Spirit, divine reality, peace, joy, power, and dominion.

Let Your Life Exemplify Truth

Do not make declarations or statements or affirmations of truth which do not fit in with your own consciousness, and expect a good result. What is the use of making such statements if your life does not conform, in some measure, to the truth you are stating? If you are permitting your consciousness to be filled with hate, anger, ingratitude, or fear, and yet sit down and give yourself a treatment by affirming: "God is love; God is life; God is all"; you will not succeed.

Nothing in all the statements you will ever make, from now until doomsday, will ever heal anyone. It is the state of consciousness in which you are living that does the healing work. It is your state of consciousness. If you are living in a state of consciousness which fears germs, wars, or depressions, you will not heal anyone of fear, lack, limitation, or disease. You will remember that we have said that Christ consciousness is your consciousness when you no longer hate, fear, or love error of any name or nature. If you are in a state of consciousness which still hates, fears, or loves error, then never think you have a healing state of consciousness, even if you can recite all the books that were ever written. Instead of learning statements of truth and then giving long treatments, make your life fit in with this truth of being. Begin to gain a conscious awareness of God's presence and power. Learn, if nothing else, to stop thinking thoughts of truth, and let God fill your thought.

You will find that to be much more powerful than any statements you have ever read in the Bible, or in all metaphysical writings, including my own. It is your state of consciousness which heals, if any healing is done and if *you* do any. It is your state of consciousness which heals when consciousness is imbued with the presence and power of God.

The Letter of Truth

Although statements of truth are of no avail, nevertheless, it is important to know the correct letter of truth. All that is necessary for you to know in so far as the letter of truth is concerned and all that is necessary for you to use in a treatment can be summed up in the following paragraphs:

1. *God:* We always begin with God. What is the nature and character of God? God is infinite intelligence. God is life, and life is immortal and eternal. God is

Spirit, incorporeal, and therefore the whole universe is incorporeal and spiritual, formed of the divine substance of being. God is principle or law; therefore, everything that exists in the world is subject to and under the government of divine law. God is the life of the individual, the mind and the Soul of the individual, the principle or law of the individual, and God is the substance of the individual. God is even the substance of the body of the individual, because the body is the temple of the living God.[11]

2. *The Nature of Individual Being:* All that God is, individual being is, whether that individual is you or I, or anybody else. All that God has, I have, and you have. "Son, . . . all that I have is thine."[12] You are not a little bit of God: All the intelligence of God is your individual intelligence; all the immortal and eternal life of God is your immortal and eternal life and being. All the Spirit and substance of God is the spiritual substance of your body, your business, and your home. All that God is, you are. All that God has, you have. Since I and the Father are one, and not two, this one includes both God and me—both God and you. All is included in this one. And in this oneness, all that God is—all that God has—is manifested as this one, which I am and which you are.

3. *The Nature of Error:* Error is nothing but a universal suggestion coming to your thought. It is the world's thought of a selfhood apart from God. It is mesmeric suggestion, a suggestion that has been so often repeated that it acts hypnotically on your consciousness and tries to use your consciousness to make you

believe that there is a selfhood or a condition apart from God. That is all there is to error, whether appearing as sin, disease, or death, or whether seeming to exist as a person. All there is to error is a universal, powerful, mesmeric belief or illusion, thrusting itself–imposing itself–upon your consciousness. If it can make your consciousness say, "I feel bad," it has won the day, and you are sick. If, instead, you instantly recognize: "None of these suggestions can reach me. I do not accept them into my consciousness as a power; and, therefore, I do not have to put them out"–you have given a treatment.

If you include these three things in your treatment–the nature of God, the nature of individual being as God manifest, and the nature of error as suggestion–that is all you will ever have to do about any discord which may come to you. That is the whole of the letter of truth, although it might be stated in many different ways. But that is all you will have to include in your treatment.

If the correct letter of truth were all that was needed to heal the world, we could dispense with all books and writings of a metaphysical nature, because, in the few paragraphs above, the truth of being is stated briefly and completely, and nothing more is needed in that respect. And yet, *one thing more is needed!* That one thing more is *your conviction of the truth*–not your declaration, but your conviction of it, your inner response to it, your actual awareness of it.

Live Truth

How can you have the consciousness that God is love, while you are hating someone, or fighting with him? You cannot have family inharmonies and, at the same time, have a healing consciousness because your very life demonstrates that you do not believe that God is love or that you are love expressed. In the same way, you cannot believe that God is infinite supply while you are dishonest in business. If your life is not in harmony with the statements you are making, do not look for any spiritual result from those statements. You just cannot say, "God is truth, and all the truth that God is, I am," and live a life of dishonesty. Your thinking that God is truth does not make it so. It is only as you become convinced that God is your supply, that God really becomes the omnipotent activity of your income and safety and security. We can no longer be unkind or dishonest, the moment we have grasped the idea that God is love and all that God is, I am.

We must gain the consciousness of these statements. Remember, I have said, "Do not use the word God so much, unless you really know what you are talking about." Sometimes, the way the word God or Christ is used is profane. One would almost as soon hear some men swear, because from a consciousness such as theirs we could perhaps expect little else. Many people, who go around talking about God or the Christ, have never seen or felt It, and they do not know what they are talking about. Certainly, they do not live It. It is a sin to claim the robe of the Christ as your consciousness, and not live up to it. As a matter of fact, such sin destroys your healing power. Let us be sure that we are not using the Truth, but that we are living Truth. Jesus did not have to give a treatment. People came into his con-sciousness, touched his Robe, and were healed. Why? There was no enmity in the state of consciousness which

Jesus had, although, sometimes, there was indignation toward the people who were calling themselves spiritual and yet living a lie.

Your consciousness is a healing consciousness when you have agreed that God is love, that love is your own being, and that God is truth, with truth the nature of the life you are living.

Become convinced that God, unfolding and acting as your individual consciousness is the only power, the only presence, reality, law, and cause, and you will then realize peace, joy, and dominion as effect.

Become convinced of your identity as life eternal, and disease and death will fall away of their own nothingness. Let your efforts not be to change the outer picture. Rather, direct your efforts toward realizing truth, love, life, as the very nature of your being.

~ 7 ~

MEDITATION

Meditation forms a most important part of our work. Although there are many ways of achieving silence and meditation, I have found only one way that meets my own need. I sit quietly, with my attention centered somewhere between the eyes and a little above, and take some word such as "life," or "God," or "Spirit," and ponder it. As my thought tries to wander, I come back gently to the same idea. I feel no sense of impatience with myself, no sense of frustration. No matter how many times the thought wanders, I bring it right back to that one word.

If you try this method, eventually, you will find that outside, intruding thoughts do not come, and you are able to sit quietly in a peaceful state of meditation. It may take days or it may take months to acquire this steadiness of mind, but it will come if you have patience and perseverance. Do not try to remain quiet for more than from three to five minutes unless you feel like it. We are doing this only for a conscious realization of our oneness, or to make our contact with God. When we have achieved that, we have achieved our purpose. We are not trying to see "light," or to have "experiences." If they come, there is nothing wrong about them. The only thing wrong would be in becoming so fascinated with these experiences that we lose our way by making too much of them.

After we have had our few minutes of meditation and have achieved the "click" or feeling of the presence of God, we get up and go about our business. If at noon, we find that we have a few minutes to use for this purpose, we repeat it; we do the same thing again at night, and in the middle of the night. Why? Because, ultimately, through providing these opportunities three or four times a day, meditation is going to become so much a part of our being that we shall be in meditation twenty-four hours a day whether awake or asleep. Then we do not have to go through a process of "healing" when someone calls upon us. We shall have been through all the preliminaries, and we shall be able to say, "Thank you, Father." Then we understand the reason for all the preliminary practice.

Ultimately, treatment becomes a very simple thing. We learn to dismiss instantly every negative suggestion that comes to us. Let us suppose that I am walking through a store and am tempted to snatch some jewelry. The thought immediately comes, "What kind of nonsense is that! Where did it come from? That temptation is no part of my nature." I walk home and that ends it. I would not treat it. I would merely keep on walking and drop the whole thing after the flash of recognition that a temptation such as this is no part of my consciousness.

Inasmuch as sin, disease, lack, and limitation are really only universal beliefs that present themselves to us for our acceptance or rejection, we must treat these by rejecting them at once. If we attach the word "I" to these and say, "I do not feel well. I am getting a cold," we have accepted the temptation or the suggestion, and an hour later or a day later we find ourselves showing forth the results of this acceptance. Suppose we had said,

"Wait a minute! Where does a thing like this come from? A temptation out of universal nothingness! I will accept no thinking like that. It is no part of the law of God and it is no part of me." We, then, would walk on, our treatment of the belief having consisted of quickly turning away from it.

I wish that all of us had the courage to adopt that form of treatment. When any temptation comes regarding ourselves or another, we should say, "Oh, no! Good-bye to you! You are temptation, suggestion, appearance; there is nothing real about you, and I am not accepting you." Then we would find quicker healing many times.

Whenever the Call to Meditate Is Felt, Meditate

It may be that sometimes while you are speaking to a person or lecturing to a group, you will find yourself impelled to stop in order to go into meditation for no human reason of which you are aware. It is not necessary that you know the reason for it. It is mind unfolding, and when your meditation is completed you can then go on with your talk or conversation. Do not be surprised to learn later that some need was met, some call was made at the instant you felt impelled to meditate. It may have been from someone you know, or it may not.

Doctors in hospitals frequently tell us that their patients "miraculously recovered" for no reason known to materia medica. Sometimes they add that "somebody must have been praying." A patient who so recovers may know the reason, because possibly he had asked for spiritual help or had some friend or relative who was working in this way. Another patient is healed just by reaching out to his concept of God. In so doing he touched the level of consciousness of someone living the spiritual life. So, even though we may not know why, we should always respond to these inner promptings for meditation and silence.

How was it possible for a man like Starr Daily, engrossed in a life of crime, suddenly to find himself so illumined as to be freed of the whole sense of sin and disease? My own thought after hearing his story was that this man, consciously or unconsciously, must have said to himself, "Oh, God! Isn't there an answer to all this? Can't I get out of this misery in some way?" Perhaps he was thinking seriously of God as God, or as some kind of Presence that could do something.

Of this we can be sure, that in his being, there was a crying out to something that appeared to him as a protective influence, a presence of Love. In doing this, he perhaps touched the consciousness of someone praying on the level of impersonal relationship and he received an answer. I am convinced there are many people who have wonderful experiences of a spiritual nature, who do not know where they have come from; they have made a contact on this plane with someone who is praying. One does not have to be praying "for" anyone; as a matter of fact, I do not think one *can* pray *for* any person. Prayer is conscious at-onement with God. Prayer is being in tune with the Infinite. Prayer is the realization of God disclosing and revealing Itself as an actual presence and power. While we are living in that state of consciousness, does not the infinity of God include anyone lifting himself into that consciousness which is so real in our thought? Why not?

When a person is trying to find some kind of God or Christ–some kind of help–with his whole being, why should he not touch your level or my level of consciousness when we are in the process of realizing and touching God, here and now? This is what happens to you when a practitioner is working for you. You do not know the minute or the hour when the practitioner is at work. You are not tuned in to any personal consciousness, nor to his "thinking." You ask for help and drop the whole matter. Sometimes you put a letter to a practitioner into the mailbox, knowing that he will not receive it for a day or for several days. But you have your healing that minute, or that hour, or six hours later. Anyway, you get it long before the practitioner receives your letter. How can this happen?

What you did was to tune yourself in to your highest sense of God consciousness, which at the moment you thought of and personalized as your practitioner. Your practitioner was living in the realization that *I* is God, and that *I* is omnipresent. Wherever and whenever someone reaches out for the unfoldment and revelation of God, he touches that Christ consciousness. A practitioner does not humanly have to know you are reaching out in order for you to receive help. You may have thought you were reaching out to Mr. Jones or Mrs. Smith, but you were not! You were reaching out to the Christ. The Christ is the practitioner's developed state of consciousness.

Is it not possible that someone else down the street, in the same moment that you reached out to God or to the Christ also reached out, touched the same Christ consciousness that you did, and had his healing? Neither of you made a human contact, for he may not have known of the practitioner, and your message may not yet have reached the practitioner. When you reach out to a practitioner for help, you must touch something higher than the thought or personality of the practitioner. You must touch that mind which was in Christ Jesus. That is where and when healing takes place.

Attain the Consciousness of God

The whole secret lies in attaining the actual consciousness, the actual feeling of God's presence. Without that feeling, we still do not have the assurance that the declarations, the affirmations, and the denials that we make are true.

You cannot fight error after you know God to be the only reality of being. You then realize that error exists as an appearance. You recognize that it exists to the ignorant sense of those not yet aware of their true identity, but that does not mean that you have to fight it. It means that you must sit at peace and realize the nothingness of it. None of this is of any importance at all—none of this truth about God and man, or about error, is of any importance—unless you get the feeling of it, unless you have the actual feeling of this Presence.

It is so easy to repeat: "My life is God. God is my life," and five minutes later begin to fear that you are going to die. It is an easy thing to make the affirmation: "I don't have to be afraid of germs, infection, or contagion. They are not power," and a few minutes later, it is just as easy to become afraid of those very things. The affirmations and the denials will not do the work. It is the feeling, the absolute conviction, the inner realization, and when it comes, it fills the whole body with a sense of reality, power, and dominion.

It is one thing to say to a little child, "Go on! Cross the street; Mother is right behind you and there is no danger." It is another thing for a mother to take the child's hand and walk across the street with him. In the first case, the child may or may not believe that there is no danger, or he may believe and still be afraid. But once he feels his mother's hand in his, all fear is gone. That is what I am trying to bring out. It is easy to say, "God is with you though you make your bed in hell." But there is no power in the words until you actually have felt God's presence when you are walking down the street, or going into a hospital to help someone.

Your words have to be God realized, God felt. Certainly, there is no presence or power apart from God, and our assurance comes when we have felt it. Over and over people ask, "Do you believe in God?" Certainly, we believe in God. But *what* do we believe? To feel God, to touch God, to have the actuality of God, is no longer to "believe" in God, *This is the experience of God.* The more you feel this, the less you can talk *about* God. We talk about It, when we ought to be able to look right up and see It. If we could, no one would have to talk about It. It should be like that with all of us. We should be able to see It and feel It, if not with the eyes, at least with our inner sense—our intuition.

God is reality. In healing or in teaching, with a patient sitting before you, it is futile to make statements or recite quotations of truth for the purpose of filling or satisfying his thought. In teaching, it is futile to memorize a lot of things from books, and then go before an audience and recite things you know nothing of, things that are not a part of your consciousness.

These statements are not power; they are nothing more than the words that come forth out of the human throat. They carry no substance and no essence. Sometimes, you may come to a period where you have nothing to say, where the answer is not there. Then, go within to God. And if it is best to say nothing, then say nothing. Let God do it. Let the work be done in silence. There is more power in a second of silence than in an hour of conversation. "The letter killeth, but the spirit giveth life."[1] So, let it come through the silence, through the Spirit, rather than through words that can be made up.

~8~

THE PRINCIPLE

Some of you are becoming aware of the fact that a principle of spiritual living and spiritual healing, different from any of the approaches that have been given to you before, is being presented to you. That does not mean that the principle involved is something new. There is nothing new about it; it is the principle revealed by Jesus Christ, as set forth particularly in the Gospel of John.

In this principle, it becomes clear to us that we do not judge the spiritual world by looking out upon the human world. Rather, we come into an awareness of what the spiritual world is, through looking out from God. "My kingdom is not of this world."[1] There is no way to judge the spiritual kingdom by looking at the appearance. When Jesus spoke of "the meat to eat that ye know not of,"[2] and of the living water, we know that he was showing forth an inner principle; one which those of the world know not, for "having eyes, see ye not? and having ears, hear ye not?"[3] Yet this is the principle which is capable of feeding, protecting, sustaining, and maintaining us.

In this approach to spiritual living and demonstration, we stay with the word God whenever we are called upon for help. We forget, immediately, the name, the body, and the disease of the so-called patient and jump at once to the word God and then go on from there. When we turn to the word God, we say, "What is God?" The answer may come back, "God is life eternal. God is Spirit, therefore incorporeal, and without material embodiment. God is Soul. God is law."

The moment that we begin to catch a slight vision of what God is, we go out from there and realize:

All that God is, I am. Therefore, am I not as incorporeal—as un-material—as God? I am as immortal and as eternal in my present embodiment as God is, since God does not cast off any embodiment or body.

If you stay in that line of consciousness, how can you accept any teaching which believes that there is a body left behind to be buried, while it—consciousness—continues to live? We are not looking at you and tracing you back to God. We are looking at God and tracing God forward to you. When we succeed in doing that, we find you to be as infinite, immortal, spiritual, incorporeal, as God Itself. When we do that, we see that we cannot leave anything; there is no place for us to go, nor anything for us to leave; we are always here as part of our own consciousness.

We cannot mix this approach with any former approach. We stand whole-heartedly with the teaching of Jesus: " 'I am the way, the truth, and the life.'⁴ All that I am as consciousness, my body is. Therefore, I can present my body to you, even after you crucify it. I can produce it for you, not as a ghost-body, but as it is, even with the nail wounds in it. A ghost has not flesh and blood as I have." In this approach, your body is really the idea or the reflection or the expression of the consciousness which you are. You are consciousness, and your body is its image and likeness. That is why, when you see me you say, "That looks like Joel Goldsmith." Certainly, my body is expressing exactly my state of consciousness. If my state of consciousness rises higher, closer to the Christ consciousness, my body will show forth a better appearance. The outer is the reflection of the inner. The inner is the real *I*, while the outer is the image or reflection or expression of it.

When we have a problem, we sit down and know the truth. Knowing the truth is a different process from making statements about the truth. For instance, someone may come to us and tell us that he has a heart condition. Our response is, "All right, what is the truth about this situation? What is the difficulty we are dealing with?" Then, beginning with God, we realize:

God is life eternal, Spirit, incorporeal. In consciousness, there is no such thing as a physical body, or an organ called a heart. Whatever is appearing as a heart or other organ is but the material or mortal concept of some divine idea or activity of life, of God Itself. God is the creative principle of Its own Being, and this Being is as spiritual as It, Itself. Therefore, all formation, all expression, must be as spiritual as the mind that conceives it.

That which mind conceives never can turn around and control mind. No formation of life can destroy life. So, if heart exists as some divine idea created by God through the instrument of the mind, how can it turn around and destroy the mind that made it? Always the action, the jurisdiction, the law, is in the mind controlling whatever it causes. Therefore, heart cannot be a law to God, to mind, to life, to the consciousness which formed it. God, the consciousness of the individual, is the law unto Its creation. This includes body as well as its organs and functions.

Now that we have recognized this truth, we sit in our silence for a little while and let it take hold in our consciousness until we feel the answering "click." That is our treatment: knowing the truth and feeling that oneness with God. We do not say, "Heart doesn't do this, or heart can't do that." We do not make a lot of statements. We forget the whole thing, unless six or twenty hours later we have not felt the benefit of it. In that event, we may sit down and ask, "What point of the realization have I missed?" Perhaps we go through a little mental process of realization, of knowing the truth, but then we let it alone.

If you try to mix this teaching with the teachings in which affirmation and denial are used as healing agencies, it will not work. Do not misunderstand me when I say this. I am not saying that those approaches are wrong, and never do I say, "This is better than that." Only this do I say, "Please try not to *mix* these different teachings." If you want this principle and teaching to work in your life, clear out the things which may conflict with it, and give it an opportunity to develop within you. Then if it is not your teaching, you will have to find another.

This is not a truth that I claim to have discovered, but it is a way of life that I have traveled, through twenty-eight years of work, watching the principle in operation during that time. Now in speaking and writing about it, I am giving you the opportunity of trying it for yourselves. All you need do is to ȯpen your consciousness to God. God reveals to you the path in which you should go. Then stay on that particular path as long as it proves to be your way.

In our approach we begin with the word God. Whatever we discover God and Its image and likeness to be, or the individualization of God to be, we acknowledge that, and then we soon begin to understand what we are, what mind is, and what expression is. Through this, we come to understand what we mean when we speak of prayer and treatment.

The procedure I have described above regarding the heart condition was a treatment. But the sitting in silence and listening gave us the inner awareness and inner confidence. When that comes from God, that is really the prayer or the "clinching" part of the treatment, and that is the part which is effective. While you are working in this way, look to God and you will find the principle. Look out from God to you, and then see that all that God is, you are.

Spiritual Integrity

Do not think, for a moment, that you can go far on this path and still lead a completely personal life. Do not think, for one moment, that once you have touched this path, you can ever go back to your old ways of living. If you should attempt to do this, you will lose the way. From the moment you touch this path, part of you is dedicated to God, part of your conscious thinking is dedicated to God. If you allow yourself to indulge in sensuousness, in hate or in fear, you are coming down from your own developed state of consciousness. You then live lower than your actual state of consciousness, and living below the level of your own consciousness is a sin against the Holy Ghost.

It is characteristic of the person knowing nothing about the Christ or Its meaning, to indulge his personal sense of greed, love, hate, or fear. He can be forgiven for that—if he knows no better! But the moment that you realize that the Christ of you is a leavening influence throughout the world, and then do not hold that light in your consciousness and do not live according to that light in your own being, you must reap the result.

In a measure, everyone who takes this path must feel himself called upon to live on a higher plane of consciousness than he did before. He cannot permit himself to indulge in the same degree of hate, fear, animosity, jealousy, or infidelity. In an ever increasing degree, he must check himself and remind himself, "No, I am maintaining this light. I have achieved a certain degree of enlightenment and I must hold that light for the benefit of the world and for myself. I cannot come down and indulge the lower instincts of existence."

I can assure you, too, that as you go higher on this path, as you reach that place where you begin to practice this, it becomes more and more apparent that you cannot live your life unto yourself, your friends, or even your family. Your life must be lived unto Christ. That becomes the first consideration and the last, and if other demands are made upon you, sooner or later you must break loose from them. These other demands may be understandable until you reach that place where you are being called upon for help.

We must become less and less concerned with giving ourselves treatments or help for supply or health. If we catch this light clearly enough, however, we shall never be without supply or health. But the error lies in taking thought for the things of this world and attempting to use this truth for personal gain. As we come to this place of spiritual unfoldment, we let all things be added to us. We do not sit down and do mental work for ourselves. We sit and consciously realize that this light is the light of the world. Our responsibility is to live as nearly as we can in accordance with our highest unfolded sense of light. Our responsibility is not to think of ourselves in personal terms, but in terms of maintaining the integrity of the message, and to let that do the work.

Think, for example, of addressing a group of businessmen, telling them about the principle that operates in business, and then having these men learn later that the person who has talked so glibly about principle has been cheating his neighbor. It does not work! Even without concrete evidence of dishonesty, the men to whom you might talk would sense it. One cannot stand up in this work living a lie and not have it reflected outwardly in some form. Inevitably, it becomes known.

Yet this does not mean that every one of us who has dedicated his life to this work has attained perfect Christhood. It means only that, insofar as motive, intent, or purpose is concerned, we live as close to this integrity as we know how. In this work, we cannot live a lie without having those we are teaching, or those to whom we are speaking or lecturing, sense it. Therefore, from the beginning, from this minute, every time you find yourself tempted to indulge in some of the lower, negative, human forms, try to lift yourself up out of it in the realization: "This is no longer my life to do with as I choose; this is the life of Christ, which is being lived for the world, to show forth the benefits of It." In this way, keep lifting yourself higher and higher in consciousness.

You can see, I trust, that in following this line of work and this mode of living, your own individual affairs will prosper, physically, mentally, morally, and financially. Yet, only as added things! Only as an out-picturing of your improved state of consciousness. Remember that the main purpose of the life you are living from this time forth, is not to improve your particular state of living with no regard for the rest of the world, but to show that your life improves as the natural unfoldment of your state of consciousness.

Becoming Instruments for the Divine Plan

As this unfoldment of consciousness continues, and as you turn within, you will find that God *is,* and that *God is Spirit.* You will find that there is a spiritual universe and a spiritual plan for that universe. Humanly, we are not living the spiritual plan; humanly, we are not a part of the divine plan. Humanly, we have separated ourselves from God. In fact, separation from the divine plan constitutes our humanhood! If we but give up our humanhood, we are no longer a part of birth, maturity, age, death, and decay: We are then part of the infinite and eternal plan, in which we can play our part unto eternity.

Now, as you turn in this life to your individual consciousness unfolding as your life, you find that you are being used more and more for a spiritual purpose. Experiences like these will come to you: You may find yourself awakening in the middle of the night, unable to go back to sleep. If you are wise and if you are earnestly following this way, you will jump up, wash your face and hands, sit down in a chair, and say, "All right, Father, here I am." Sit there in peace and quiet; let the Father work out Its plan through your consciousness. At that moment, you may, and then again you may not, know what part you are to play in the divine plan. Even though that may not be revealed to you at this time, something is being worked out on the spiritual level of consciousness, something is taking place when you are awakened at night. Do not dismiss such wakefulness as mere insomnia. Realize that it is a call from God and get up so as to make yourself available as an instrument. This may not happen only at night; it may happen in the middle of the day, and when it does, be willing to go off into a corner as soon as you can to realize your oneness with God:

All that God is, I am. My oneness with God constitutes my oneness with the entire universe. Therefore, I am an instrument for all the good of God, and it flows out to all who are reaching out for it.

You become an instrument of the divine plan in proportion as you accept the call that comes to you from within. You will know it when it comes; you will not mistake it. It is a pull, a tug, sometimes even a physical tug. You will recognize it as a call to go off by yourself and sit down to meditate. It may have something to do with your own affairs and may result in your receiving some healing, warning, guidance, cautioning, or preparation, or it may have nothing to do with you. It may be the activity of the divine plan in operation.

This book began with the statement that God is infinite, divine consciousness, unfolding, disclosing, revealing Itself, manifesting and expressing Itself as your individual consciousness. Then, is it not a normal and natural thing to know and to realize that the God, which is your individual consciousness, is "about the Father's business," not only for you, but for the whole universe? How can God be your mind, and your mind be continuously engaged only in concern about your personal affairs? If you accept God as the divine, infinite, universal consciousness, acting, operating, and appearing as your individual consciousness, then be prepared to have your consciousness serve a purpose for the benefit of mankind. This work is the surrender of the self to the universal Self. It is the surrender of one's personal sense of life to the purpose of the divine life.

Let us begin to realize a little more fully the statement we have used as our banner: God is infinite consciousness, infinitely disclosing, unfolding, revealing, expressing, and manifesting Itself as our individual consciousness. Let us begin to see what is expected of us who have the mind of Christ Jesus. Can we be personal or limited after that? If it is really true that God is our mind, how are we acting out here in the world? Are we humanly living up to that consciousness which we are?

Why do you think that we are in the world, if God is our individual consciousness? Is it too much to expect another Jesus on earth when every one of us has "the mind that was in Christ Jesus?" We could have twenty or thirty people with the mind of Christ Jesus, if enough of us could realize:

I am not living a little, personal, finite life. Inasmuch as God is expressing Itself as my life, as my being, as my consciousness, then infinity is flowing out from me. Anyone in the world who touches me, is automatically healed or reformed because of that touch—because God is disclosing, unfolding, revealing Itself, and is appearing as my individual consciousness.

Why should not a person be able to touch God and be healed and reformed? And if God is our individual consciousness, why should not coming within range of our consciousness produce this healing influence? Is that not the teaching of Jesus Christ in the New Testament? How could a woman who pressed through the throng and touched the hem of his robe be healed? Was it because of Jesus? No, he said "It is the Father within who doeth the works." He knew that God was the infinite awareness, the infinite consciousness, of his being.

Do you see what we are doing to ourselves as we continue in our selfish, personal way of life, living only unto ourselves, our friends, and our families? Do you not see that we have set limitations on ourselves? We should have learned that God is individual mind, the only mind of this universe, and that we should persist in our efforts to leave behind our selfish mode of life and accept infinity as the measure of our life. Whose fault is it that we have not accepted this? Ours! Instead of taking books and using them as textbooks for a greater understanding, we have read them with the superstitious hope that by the time we have finished them, we would be healed. How many times have we been told, "If you will just read this book long enough, you will get your healing," or, "If you will learn the affirmations in this book, you will be healed?" That is what has been happening; but if instead of that, we were to take a book and say, "What statement of truth is here that is the truth of my being?" we would find truth in every book we read.

We do not even have to go so far. Emerson told us that God is the universal mind, that this mind is the mind of individual man, and that every man is an inlet to that same mind, and to all of the same. That is what we are saying here. We are the inlet and the outlet for the whole of the activity of the mind of God. So, if you speak of the mind that was in Christ Jesus, you have really spoken of your mind, your Soul, your consciousness.

Therefore, if you think that Jesus could heal and reform on this earth, you should know that you, yourself, should be able to do the same, since the same mind that was in him is in you. Of course, only to the degree that we have overcome physical sense, is the mind of God our mind. It could not function for us as demonstration, or as an activity or avenue of demonstration, except in proportion as we individually have become purged of personal sense, that is, of our hate, love, and fear of error. The mind that was in Christ Jesus is the mind of all people walking up and down the earth, but it is of no avail to them unless and until they consciously purge their thought or mind of its fear, hate, and love of error.

Consciousness Is Supply

Let us again use the illustration of money. One way of purging ourselves, and thereby manifesting the mind that was in Christ Jesus, is to look at money—whether it be a quarter or a hundred dollars—and ask ourselves, "What is it?" Then we start with the understanding that as matter it is only a concept. In the United States it happens to be an American concept. In Germany, it is a different concept, and in England, still different. At best, as a piece of matter, it is only a concept, and its value varies and changes. But, as a symbol of a spiritual idea, it represents exchange; it represents value. It may represent an avenue of gratitude. However, even in its spiritual significance, it is an effect. An effect of what? Of the mind of God, divine Consciousness. Is there at any time any power in this money, or even in the idea which it represents? Is there any value in it? Or is the power and the value in the consciousness that formed it?

As we use these illustrations, we come again to the orange or the lemon tree. You can now say: "How grateful I am that I do not believe that the supply is in the orange or the lemon, but rather that it is in the life appearing as the orange or the lemon tree which produces this fruit. So long as I have the life as the tree, the fruit will come forth. Never shall I put the value in the orange itself." Again, we can go back to money and say: "I am grateful to see that this exists as an effect just as much as does the orange on the tree. That which gives it life is the consciousness that forms it, and that is God consciousness, my own individual consciousness."

If I place money on a table, it is dead, inert, and it remains dead. It cannot go to you, and it cannot come to me. Even if it is a million dollars, it is still inert–dead. Something has to happen in your consciousness, or in mine, to start its flow to you or to me. That something is our consciousness which is the law of attraction unto that which is appearing as effect. The moment you grasp this, you no longer have an attachment for oranges or for dollars. You no longer hate, fear, or love them. You see them for what they are–a medium of exchange. You understand that *I*, the consciousness of my being–God, the divine Consciousness of me–is the law unto that

medium of exchange, and as long as I have that consciousness, these things will keep on being attracted to me.

In the degree that you see this vision, you have the
mind that was in Christ Jesus on the subject of supply. If
you catch this, you have the mind of Christ Jesus insofar
as it applies to supply, and you find yourself able to meet
any and every normal, natural demand made upon you,
even if you need food for a crowd of five thousand.
Remember, if you look in your pocketbook, you may
not find any money there. But if you realize that the
demand is not being made upon your pocketbook, but
upon your consciousness, that your consciousness is
God, and that, therefore, your consciousness is infinite,
you will have all you can want or need.

The Issues of Life Are in Consciousness

Let us take a further step: Let us consider the organs
and the functions of our body. Up to the time of our
coming into metaphysics, we believed that the issues of
life were in the body: The heart, we thought, might
destroy our life; the lungs might affect our health, and,
ultimately, our life. But, in spiritual teaching, the first
thing we are told and which we find to be true is that
God is the only power, and that there is no action or
power in the body in and of itself.

At some period in your development, you must
accept these statements as truth and say to yourself:
"Why am I afraid of a heart, a liver, or a lung, if the
action or the intelligence of them is the mind that
formed them? I will never fear what organs or functions
can do to me. What difference does it make what is
going on any place in the body? If consciousness is

controlling the body, then consciousness is the only thing with which I am concerned."

To have the mind that was in Christ Jesus on the subject of health means to have the conscious awareness that the issues of life are in your consciousness, not in the organs and functions of your body. Then, as you learn not to hate, fear, or love money, you will learn not to hate, fear, or love the organs and functions of the body, for you will know:

God, the mind of me, is the law unto everything appearing as my body. God, the mind of me, is the law unto the spiritual idea operating as body. My awareness of this acts on this concept called the physical body.

This form, which is visible to the eyes, is not my body. It is the universal concept of the body that God created. This concept is governed in accordance with the degree of truth that I know about God and the spiritual body. The truth that I know about God, and God's government of the spiritual body, becomes operative as my understanding, controlling this concept of body.

So then, in order to have the mind that was in Christ Jesus so far as healing works are concerned, it is impossible, by looking at the body, to release the healing power, since the issues are not in the body or in the muscles, but are in consciousness governing the muscles, organs, or functions of the body. You must purge yourself of the universally accepted belief of the body as governing life and accept the truth that life governs the body. You must make an absolute reversal of the world-belief that the heart, stomach or lungs control life.

You do not acquire the mind that was in Christ Jesus by going to church; you do not get it by praying on your knees, nor do you get it by giving ten percent of your income to a church. You have the mind of Christ Jesus by a conscious realization that God is the mind of you, and that God is the mind of your body and business, and that that mind controls its own formation, which is spiritual being and spiritual body. Through this understanding, you are a law unto this concept of body.

Any one of us can have the mind that was in Christ Jesus on the subject of supply, health, or harmony, but only in the degree to which we can bring ourselves not to hate, love, or fear the organs and functions of the body, or money, or error of any and every form and nature.

We are living the life of the Master in the degree in which we absorb these teachings of the Master, and we must do it consciously. We cannot sit around and wait for the mind of God to come down and do something for us. We must lift ourselves into a conscious awareness of God's government of Its universe and, at the same time, stop loving, hating, or fearing error of any name or nature—stop fearing anything or anybody in the external world, that is, in the world of effect.

Jesus had this understanding so highly developed that he did not even acknowledge that it took earth or land to support his weight. The higher we go, the more we understand that it is Consciousness, God, that supports, maintains, and sustains us. And it is the same God, whether we are in the air, on land or on water.

Looking at a twenty-five cent piece, I could very well think, "You won't support me for very long." But, suppose I think of the Spirit that animates and forms that quarter. Will not that Spirit support me? Yes, unto eternity! Any grossness, any materiality consists in looking for support to the twenty-five cent piece, instead of to the Spirit which animates it. Our grossness and our materiality continue while we look to the organs and the functions of the body to maintain and sustain us, instead of realizing: "I know! The Spirit that formed this body is the same Spirit that sustains it unto eternity." Now we can understand why Jesus said: "I have meat to eat that ye know not of . . .[5] whosoever drinketh of the water that I shall give him shall never thirst; but the water that I shall give him shall be in him a well of water springing up into everlasting life."[6] If you drink of the water that I give you, it will be unto you a wellspring of water. Why? Because, as we realize that we are not living on food or vitamins, and that we do not live by bread alone, we are fed from within; we are eternal.

To our present sense, we need bread, but that is not what is maintaining us for from sixty to one hundred years. We are being fed by this understanding from within. The same Spirit which animates the dollar, animates also the body. The same Spirit, that animated our body at ten years or at thirty years, can animate it at a thousand years of age. If it is Spirit that animates and sustains us at ten or at thirty, it must be Spirit that can animate us at one thousand years of age. If this is not true, the atheist is right—we are just pieces of machinery that wear out. We have adopted the teaching, or religion, or philosophy—call it by what name you will—which says: "We live not by bread alone, but by the Spirit of God." We are not fed, nor are we harmed by what goes into the mouth, but by that which comes out of consciousness.

In every area of our experience, we turn to the teaching of the Master for guidance. In the field of human relations, we take the Master's teaching: "Who is my mother, or my brethren? . . . Whosoever shall do the will of God, the same is my brother, and my sister, and mother."[7] Need we, then, continue to live our lives in slavish devotion to blood relatives, regardless of whether or not they are on the path of our own unfoldment? Or should our life be so lifted that a pathway is opened permitting us to follow our own sense of unfoldment? As we learn to love our neighbor as ourselves, we will not cast off our relatives or friends, but we will maintain our own identity. We do this by living according to our highest concept of life, according to our own idea of unfoldment, and by spending as much time as we can in the company of those who are on our path.

~9~

THE CHRIST

The purpose of this message is to set you free through a spiritual awareness of your oneness with God. If you find your oneness with God, you will need no contact with "man, whose breath is in his nostrils."[1] This whole message is a statement, or restatement, of your oneness with God now—with or without material organization or human contacts.

The Christ is a feeling or recognition of a Presence within your consciousness; It is something that transcends human experience, but which, at the same time, enriches human experience. Christ is a divine reality! It is the power or presence of God, infinite, complete, whole. It is part of your consciousness. Actually, it may constitute the whole of your consciousness, depending upon the degree of your unfoldment. It is beyond description in human terms.

Christ is a presence and power beyond your human ability to realize. It can be discerned only through your developed spiritual sense, because it takes something far greater than the brain or intellect to perceive the Christ. It takes spiritual awareness, spiritual alertness, and that comes in proportion as the world means less and less to you. The coming of the Christ makes this world, the world of concept, an unreality. It decreases dependence on anything in the realm of things or of thoughts.

The Christ is Spirit. It is that Spirit which transcends things and thoughts. In the presence of the Christ, it is not necessary to entertain a thought. And yet that same Christ fills us with thoughts emanating from the infinite Intelligence, the infinite Wisdom, the divine Love that is really the center of our being. Christ is the healing influence in our experience. Christ is the saving influence. Christ is the guiding, directing, maintaining, and sustaining influence in our experience—and all without our taking a thought. "Which of you by taking thought can add to his stature one cubit?[2] ... [Or can] make one hair white or black?"[3]

In the degree, then, that you are able to transcend human thinking and look through the world of appearances, feeling little or no sense of hate, love, or fear for it or from it, or dependence upon it, in that degree, are you entertaining the Christ in your consciousness.

The Birth of the Christ

In our human experience, we celebrate Christmas, which symbolizes the birth of the Christ. The Christ comes not only on December 25th; the Christ may come at any moment of your experience. It may come, as a very first appearing, in a moment of great distress. It depends upon you. It depends upon how much you have overcome self, and how much you have opened your consciousness to this Christ. The Christ is always immaculately conceived and always brought forth in virginity, in the mind that is prepared to give up its material sense of existence.

The Christ does not come where there is a great deal of the personal self—selfishness, self-pity, or self-righteousness.

Usually, the Christ comes to one who, in some measure, is willing to say, "This is not so much a matter of me or mine. It is a matter of transcending this human experience and rising above the joys as well as the sorrows of sense." In that degree of spiritual consciousness, the Christ is born. Jesus, the Christ, was born in a manger. The manger of old was the least desirable part of the entire establishment. The manger was outside. It was used by cattle and other domestic animals, and not as a place for human beings to inhabit. Just so, is the Christ always born in human thought, and that is about as low a place as we can reach in our individual experience. Why? Because all human thought is based on "I," "me," "mine." All human thought is based on getting, acquiring, achieving, and accomplishing.

The Christ, however, even though It is born into that kind of an atmosphere, soon dispels it; even a manger can become a holy place. So all human thought, when imbued with the Christ, becomes holy. Then, instead of the old sense of "I," "me," "mine," of getting, achieving, accomplishing, desiring, wanting, and longing for something, we find within ourselves a great sense of love, a great sense of joy and freedom, a great desire just *to be*. And that manifests itself in a healing consciousness. You never find a Christ consciousness without Its being a healing influence. The moment that the Christ touches you, you become a healer; in what degree, you determine by the manner in which you entertain the Christ.

When the Christ is born in human consciousness it must be carefully nurtured. That Jesus entertained the Christ without measure is evidenced by his healing ministry. The more we know about his life and background, the more shall we be able to understand his message and his mission. The question arises as to whether or not Jesus received his early instruction in India. There is no definitive answer to this. Each one is entitled to his opinion. From my own study, I am convinced that Jesus was a member of the Essenes, an organization which knew the secret of the mysteries, that is, the secret of spiritual healing. The Essenes walked on the water, walked through walls, multiplied the loaves. They could bring gold out of the earth, and they knew all of the spiritual, occult mysteries.

The Essenes undoubtedly had their origin in India, and their teaching was based on the mysteries and the teaching of the Hindus. In Jesus' time, some of the Essenes lived and worked in Jerusalem and throughout the Holy Land, and it is my own conviction that Jesus must have encountered one of these mystics in his early childhood. Probably, because his consciousness lent itself to it, he was introduced into the work and his great understanding came about, first, through the Essene Order, and then, later, through enlightenment.

Authority for the assumption that Jesus went to India to learn the mysteries is that in some of the monasteries of India there are written records with the name "Jesus" in them. I have never been able to accept that as conclusive authority, because we know that the Man of Galilee was not named "Jesus" until long years after his crucifixion. Jesus is a Latin or Greek name. Jesus, himself, however, was a Hebrew, and his language was Aramaic. His name probably was either Joshua or one of the similar names of that period. I am sure that at no time in his career, had you addressed him as "Jesus," would he have known that you were speaking to him. There was no such a name as "Jesus" in the Holy Land. Being a

Greek name, it could come only through translation of the name "Joshua."

Jesus never would have recognized himself, either, under the name "the Christ." There is no such word in the Aramaic language. The Aramaic word for savior is Messiah. So, as he traveled up and down the Holy Land, he might have been known as Joshua, the Messiah. When that was translated into Latin and Greek, it became Jesus, the *Christus* or *Christos;* and in English, that becomes Jesus, the Christ.

When records in India showing the name "Jesus," are pointed out, I cannot believe that that name refers to a man named "Joshua," who probably never knew the Latin or the Greek language. Paul knew Greek and Latin; Paul was a citizen of Rome; but Jesus was a Galilean. He was of the Holy Land and of the Hebrew people, with a pure Hebrew background. We have no knowledge of Jesus' using any language other than his own.

In India, there is a widely accepted teaching that we are Soul, that we are Spirit, but that we inhabit a material body. I doubt whether Jesus, had he accepted that teaching, would have been able to free himself sufficiently from it to accept the immortality of the body, as well as the immortality of the Soul. We know that Jesus accepted the immortality of the body, because he returned with his body, in the same body. That would not have been a part of the Hindu teaching. "A spirit hath not flesh and bones, as ye see me have."[4] He returned in the same body of flesh and blood.

There are three great teachers of the Orient: Lao-Tse about 600 B.C.; Buddha about 550 B.C.; Shankara, 200 or 300 B.C. All revealed the nature of God as *I Am.*

Moses, of course, had realized this truth long before any of these teachers. Of all of them, it remained for Jesus to acknowledge the immortality of the body, to acknowledge that even the body cannot be destroyed. For that reason, in my opinion, he went a step beyond all the rest; and that was because he did not have the background of oriental teaching to transcend. Jesus seems to have been particularly free of all orthodox teachings. He was free even of some of the old teachings of the Hebrew church.

Let us, in our work, hold as one-pointedly as we know how, to the truth of God as the actual life, mind, being, and body of individual you and me. When once we acknowledge God to be the reality of being, we have done away with the need for observing rituals, ceremonies, or creeds, or for celebrating holy days. All we have to do is to learn to live in the consciousness of our present perfection. Let us live in the constant realization of our true identity. After we have done that, there is only one other step, and that is to realize that the errors of the world, all of those things that the world is fighting, are not errors at all; they are illusions. And then, let us learn not to fight them, not to try to subdue or overcome them, or even try to get rid of them. Let us learn to live in a beautiful state of peace, the peace that comes from the understanding of God as the only reality of being.

Effects of the Christ

The Christ is always a gentle influence. From the moment It appears in our lives, we lose the ability to be very angry or very selfish. The Christ is made manifest in a gentleness of attitude toward those with whom we come in contact. The Christ is the greatest sense of forgiveness the world has yet known. That is the reason Jesus places so much stress on forgiving our enemies, praying for our enemies, forgiving and praying for those who despitefully use us, forgiving seventy times seven, forgiving every day those who seek it.

The Christ, once It is received, cannot bear ill will, or hold enmity or antagonism even toward those who hate It. Do you remember Jesus' response to human hate: " 'Put up again thy sword into his place: for all they that take the sword shall perish with the sword.'[5] No one can destroy or hurt me, since I am life eternal. This is an opportunity to prove that anyone or anything calling himself or itself a hater of truth, a hater of love, is not a power. It is a balloon, ready for a pin to be stuck into it. So put up your sword. I will prove that they can do nothing. Those that live by the sword shall perish by the sword. Those who believe that error is so real that they must go out and do battle with it and reform it, will perish by their own belief in a power and a presence apart from God. The Christ always says, 'Father, forgive them; for they know not what they do.'[6] "

As you come to know the Christ in your consciousness and, through this understanding, arrive at the place where your criticism is not as strong as once it was, your feelings about "I," "me," "mine," and your feelings about conditions and circumstances will become less fearful or personal than they were formerly.

The Christ is a leavening influence. It carries us from the levels of material consciousness to those levels which are more nearly spiritual. Ultimately, It lifts us into that which is true Spirit. Therefore, It is forever operating in our consciousness as an uplifting and a purifying influence.

You can determine the degree to which you are absorbing It and responding to It, by watching the degree to which you are losing your fear, your hatred, and your love of materiality, of sensuality, of sensuousness, or of grossness in any form.

The degree of the Christ that is making Itself manifest in our consciousness may be determined by the degree in which we are losing our taste for the common and the ordinary, and by the degree in which It lifts our consciousness up to greater appreciation of good literature, music, art, in short, all the cultural aspects and refinements of life. The Christ always translates Itself to our consciousness in terms of human betterment. That is why the Christ interpreted Itself as loaves and fishes for the five thousand. That is why the Christ manifested Itself in physical, mental, and moral healings.

The Christ always interprets Itself in terms of better humanhood—as a higher, individual demonstration of good. You can usually tell to what degree the Christ is operating in your consciousness by the degree of improved health that you are experiencing, the increased sense of supply, and the increased sense of better human relationships. If your friends, your relatives, and your employer or employees like you better, the Christ is being manifested in visible form in your experience. We can mark our own progress on this path by the degree of the improved sense of living that we are showing forth, by the degree of an improved sense of pleasures, pastimes, and reading matter we are enjoying.

The Christ, although invisible and even intangible to human sense, is very evident in effect, and very evident *as effect.* We can learn consciously to feel and to know the Christ, and one thing is certain, we shall know Its presence by Its results—and the results will always be good. There is no such thing as entertaining the Christ in consciousness and not having the fruitage of it. If the fruitage is not there, then the Christ is not there, even though you may think It is. Although you may think you are making the effort, your effort has not yet been successful. You may be on the way, or you may have mistaken the path and have to retrace your steps and learn wherein you have failed. Why? Because the presence of the Christ is manifest as the presence of improved conditions in our individual experience, and It never fails.

It is that which, as the Christ, became the consciousness of Saul of Tarsus, and yet it was nine years before he came forth in his Christ consciousness to travel, lecture, preach, and heal. So, too, the entrance of the Christ in our consciousness may not manifest Itself the very next day in perfect human conditions. There may be that period of readjustment when the Christ is active and operating in consciousness and is gradually overcoming the fears of sense, the hates of sense, the personalities of sense—the personal discords of mind, body, and morals.

The Christ is very real. The moment It touches you, you are aware of It. It can come as It has to many in one blinding flash, or It can come as It did to John, as a gradual unfoldment of the Christ in consciousness, a gradual unfolding of thought and of the light of Truth, made manifest as spiritual vision or spiritual apprehension.

John so clearly entertained the Christ, or received the Christ, that when he looked out on the universe, he saw the temple of God not "made with hands."[7] He saw the divine realities of being. He saw God's creation, and he knew that there was "no night there."[8] There were no sins there. There were no diseases there. There was no death there. All these had been overcome through the discernment of the Christ in his consciousness.

Did he look out and see a world "out here" suddenly become perfect? No! The whole history of the world shows that there is no such thing as a world that has attained perfection at any time. Therefore, neither you nor I will ever be able to look out and say, "The world has become perfect." You and I will behold the perfect universe only as an extension, as an activity of our own consciousness. It will be our own consciousness that will be the temple not "made with hands," in which there will be no material structure, and in which we shall have realized the spiritual body, the spiritual home, and the spiritual marriage. All will be taking place in and of our consciousness. The only effect upon the world will be that that part of the world which can see and understand us will partake in a measure of that same vision.

If you can grasp one little grain of the fact that God is actually your own consciousness, that God is appearing as your individual consciousness; if you can catch one grain of that, you will begin to discern, in your consciousness, the temple not "made with hands." You will begin to see that God is really the mind and Soul of you. You, too, will see the Christ, because your consciousness, which is God, will be manifesting Itself to you as a world not "made with hands," a world eternal in your consciousness. And when that comes to you, you will have a universe that will never be taken from you—a home, a wife, a husband, a child, and supply that you can never lose—because it will be your own consciousness appearing as form.

That one statement—God is your own consciousness. If you can grasp one little bit of that one statement, you have the Christ right in your hands. You have the whole secret of living right in your hands when you know that everyone is mind or consciousness attracted to you in form. Even my telling you this is your own spiritual development made manifest in the form of a man. The whole world of Truth is embodied in those few words! It only requires discernment, inner vision, a development of the spiritual sense to see that when you close your eyes and say *I,* you are saying God:

God made this universe and God appears to me as the forms necessary to my unfoldment. My oneness with God constitutes my oneness with every spiritual idea. It makes no difference where that idea is at this moment. My oneness with every spiritual idea is so much a part of spiritual law that at the moment a need appears to me, fulfillment will be there.

The Coming of the Christ to Human Consciousness

The Christ, this great truth, comes to your human awareness. It is said that the Christ is born in the manger, but that manger is your human awareness. What happens, then, to your human awareness? It begins to be dispelled. It becomes volatilized. This Christ, this great truth of the infinite Presence and Power, comes to you while you are yet depending on "man, whose breath is in his nostrils."[9] It comes to you while you are yet depending on human government and organization. It comes to you in some degree while you are depending on dollars and investments, and in some degree while you are yet depending on medicine. It comes to you and

It says: "Entertain Me a little while, and watch these other things disappear. Then, soon, you will begin to love Me for My own sake, and not for the loaves and fishes."

Sometimes when this Christ comes to our consciousness, we have to take it "down into Egypt." We have to hide it. We all have friends and relatives who want to get their hands on It. They will attempt to show us the "error" in ourselves and in the world. They do not see that we have come forth nearly ninety percent from the "old man" that we were, and that we are grateful for this much progress and can afford to be patient in attaining the remaining ten percent. Our friends and our relatives see only that we do not like to play cards any more, or that we no longer enjoy drinking, or that we do not care to spend so much of our time at the movies. They do not realize that we have come into something higher and more satisfying. So we must carry our Christ into "Egypt." We have to live in the world, but not be of it.

In some cases we must conform to the standards of human existence, even while, within our own being, we realize that this phase of our existence is over. And so we gratefully come out of "Egypt." We come back with our Christ. Ultimately, we come out into the open with It. But when we do, we receive a great shock. We find that we are in a temple which we thought was holy ground, only to find the "moneychangers" there, and we say, "What is this I have been a part of?" And out comes the old whip. That is bad business because we are resorting to force, and even Jesus did not succeed in purifying the temple by means of force. It is true that in subsequent years some attempts that were made to reform the church succeeded, but many others failed.

No human organization—religious, political, or commercial—can be purified unless that purification comes about as the result of the transformation of the consciousness of those comprising the organization.

No business has more integrity than the consciousness of the man or group of men who own it. No president in our government will ever bring more integrity into that government than he has in his own being. It is the same with church government, and Jesus found that out. He started to drive the "moneychangers" out, but they came right back. We have all been through certain phases of church work, and have found that for a year, or perhaps for three years, our church has manifested a goodly degree of the divine reality, has really shown forth the principle for which it stood. Then came a new board, or a new leader, and the old "situations" were right back again.

And so after we have tried our best to purify the temple and found that it did not work, we go out from the temple, and preach by the wayside. We preach wherever our voice will find a listener, whether by a roadside, on a mountain top, in a field, or by the side of the sea. Like Paul, we do not care whether we go to the Gentiles or to the Hebrews. We carry the message to anyone who will listen, in the hope that here and there someone will catch the vision. And we learn that the Christ comes only to that consciousness that is prepared for it.

Crucifixion

All the rooms at the inn were filled: There was only one little manger that was ready for the birth of the

Christ. Here is one, and there is one, who is ready, anxious for something better than sensuous living. Many others hear the words, but only those who have ears to hear and eyes to see, hear and see the message. So the Christ goes up and down the shores of Galilee, into and out of Jerusalem. The human being who is beginning to entertain the Christ has both mountain top experiences and valley experiences. When it comes to the valley experiences, that is where most of us fail in our progress. We dislike the valley experiences, and we become impatient with them. If we had studied thoroughly the life of the Master, we would remember that although he went up to the mountain top and had the experience of transfiguration—probably the highest demonstration ever attained on earth—he also went to the foot of the mountain, and there healed and fed the multitudes, not only once, but a second time, and then rebuked them for their lack of understanding of the principle.

Had Jesus promised us that the Christ Way was an easy way, we should know by now that we are all on the wrong path, for we are not finding it easy. We are having trials and tribulations, always of a varied nature. Yet once the problem of a diseased body has been surmounted through our realization of the Christ, we do not have too many of such experiences. We might have a cold, or wear glasses for a while, but that is so unimportant. Our spiritual sense of health carries us forward, and this or that little annoyance does not bother us too much.

In the same way, once we have worked out the problem of supply in our own consciousness, through the realization of the Christ, we do not have to worry again. We may have periods when we do not have an over-abundance of supply, but we have learned that "manna" falls "day by day"; we do not care whether our bank account is or is not equal to tomorrow or the day after tomorrow. We have overcome the fear of money—the fear of the lack of it—and the fear of tomorrow. Even if circumstances should take us through periods of limitation, we can be assured that once we have touched the Christ, we no longer need have any concern or worry about them, and only rarely after that do we know lack or limitation. Health and poverty are relative things and a person who has even a slight understanding of any of the spiritual teachings in the world, is not bothered too much about whether he has ten dollars or ten thousand dollars. He knows that in either case, it is only an incident of today, because he has caught some measure of understanding of what the presence and power of the Christ in his consciousness can do.

Even Jesus had his Gethsemane, and so do we. We have the valley experiences, but we also go to the Mount of Transfiguration. Occasionally, we get up there and actually behold the world of reality. And when we do, it is the most glorious experience in the world! There is not a practitioner, not a single individual who, having once been the instrument for healing someone, has not caught some measure of the vision of the Mount of Transfiguration.

We who travel this path do have experiences that would, if we accepted them as reality, drag us down utterly. But at most they are temporary experiences. So let us learn not to take too seriously the ills that come "for a day." Sometimes these ills may be blessings. When we reach that state of consciousness which sees the oranges as fruit and not as supply—as the fruit of supply—then, we never again can know a financial problem.

The ills of the flesh, or of the body, will continue to come in some degree until we reach the realization of spiritual health and body—that place in consciousness where we can look at these things with no desire and with no concern. As we come into the state of consciousness which knows that the organs and functions of the body have nothing at all to do with our life—that it is really our life or consciousness that is governing the organs and functions of the body—we shall use these problems to push us higher and higher into God-realization. When we no longer have problems of our own body, they will come to us by way of our patients' bodies. But we must be able to "handle" our own first. And these will keep coming into our thought in one form or another, until we arrive at that state of consciousness that can say, "None of these things moves me. I know that the power of life and death is not in the world of effect, but in the word of God—in consciousness."

Do not ever forget that the Master was *learning* in the three-year period of his ministry. It took those three full years before he was able to say: "He that seeth me seeth him that sent me."[10] He went through the period, first, of being a son of man, then, a Son of God, and finally he realized: "I am He, and besides Me there is none other." So it was with all of the great prophets. All of them went through the period of being human prophets, prophesying human events, before they came into the vision of spiritual reality.

When you follow Jesus along his path of healing, you are impressed with the fact that he did not set up a healing ministry; that is, he did not establish branches of truth teaching, centers in which were practitioners to do the healing work; nor did he help the disciples to become established in one city after another so that they could perform the miracles of loaves and fishes.

What he did was to set forth the principle, and then he left that for those who could catch it to live by. He preached it and hoped that all the world could and would receive it, although within himself he probably knew better. He knew the excuses human beings make not to come. He knew the boredom that can come with hearing the same message over and over, dressed up in different words. He knew all of the ways in which the human mind can be sidetracked, and he was prepared for them, remembering that "My sheep hear my voice."[11]

Paul, too, went out into the service of healing the world, and you need only read his letters to the churches to know his tribulations. He was determined to make Christians of all of them, and you cannot make a Christian of anybody. God, working in individual consciousness, leads a person, in the moment of his readiness, to the Christ–to the teacher or to the teaching which is for him. Then he knows, "This is it!" and seizes it. From that moment on, It starts to develop, unfold, externalize, and reveal Itself as individual consciousness.

The message presented in these pages would go on even should I decide to retire tomorrow and live up in the mountains or by the seaside. Nothing can stop this message because it is of the Christ. It does not need me. It has never needed me. It would have come into existence whether I led myself to it or not because somebody else would have led himself into it. That is the mission of this Christ. It will always find a "manger" in which to be born, and then it will go out into the world in the form of a human being. If one person does not take up the work, another one will.

If you feel that this is your message and that it is your responsibility to carry it to the world, you may suffer crucifixion. But it will be your own error that will crucify you because this is not your message: This is the Christ message. We suffer crucifixion in the degree to which we personalize the message. We can suffer crucifixion in another way, also. We can personalize the evil in another person's life. If we personalize the evil which makes of this man a thief, or of that man an alcoholic, or of another diseased or dead, it will come back to us. When they tried to personalize the Christ and sought to worship Jesus, his answer was, "Why callest thou me good?" When you deify a person, personalize a message, or personalize evil, you may be crucified, but you will have crucified yourself. You will have crucified your own harmonious sense of things, and you will have been the one who brought it all onto your own shoulders.

When you give out a message, say, "This is the message; it is yours to have, or not, as you choose." Then there will be no crucifixion for you. You are not claiming personal ownership of the message. If anyone wants to hate it or crucify it, he will not be touching any person. All the crucifixion that will ever come will come to the Christ, to the Truth Itself, and the Truth knows how to dissolve it. The only answer the Christ has to persecution and crucifixion is, "Put up thy sword. You cannot do anything to me. I will prove eternal life on or off the cross."

If you can visualize yourself as Truth and Life and Love, how can anyone or anything touch you or reach you with a material whip—whether that whip be a thing or a thought? Is crucifixion not dependent upon your acceptance of the belief that you are a person, instead of that you are life eternal? Once you know that you are consciousness, let them try to nail you—consciousness—to a cross! Try to entomb consciousness! When you see that point, you are another step farther from ever passing on.

Remember that every experience of the Christ takes you farther and farther away from age, decomposition, and death. In the Garden of Gethsemane, Jesus found that he was alone with God. No one was with him. In the deepest experience that you ever have to go through, you also will find that you are alone. No one can help you through these experiences, even though he may sit with you all night. In a roomful of people, still are you alone.

But you and your individual awareness of your true identity will save you. There may be six practitioners sitting around your bedside, but when it comes to the final demonstration, all of them together will not carry you through. They can do a great deal for you up to a certain point, and then it is you, yourself, who will enter heaven with the Christ.

Remember the thief on the cross? In his last agony, he turned to the Christ to bring him through the experience. Probably up to that moment, he had been depending on the weapons of the world; but in the last minute he had only the Christ, and he had sufficient wisdom to turn to That in his last mortal strife and to pray to be taken into heaven. So with us. We, too, in our human sense, are thieves, thieves of time. But one day we come to a place where no human agency can carry us through, and then we have to turn to the Christ, because only the Christ is the divine, spiritual presence and power of God in our consciousness. And we, in our human sense of lack and limitation, will suffer and will turn to that and will find the answer there.

Let the Christ Interpret Itself

Every one of the experiences that we encounter in our own human existence, can be found in Scripture. Notice how Paul organized the church, and how he had to scold people and find fault with them, showing them the error of their ways. I bring this out merely to show that when you attempt to mix the Christ, which is incorporeality, with the corporeal, you are in trouble. You cannot organize the Christ, and by that I do not refer only to church organization. You cannot organize the Christ as a physical body, or you will set up one member against another. You will have the mind warring with the flesh, and the flesh with the bones, and the bones with the blood. The Christ is incorporeal being, and until you can see yourself as incorporeal, you will be fighting the warfare between the Spirit and the flesh; you will be trying to use God, incorporeal Spirit, to patch up the organized mass of flesh called a physical body.

It is impossible to have peace in a church organization, or to have peace in a physical body. Either one is a Tower of Babel. If you accept the Christ in your consciousness, you must take the next step also and see that the embodiment or body of the Christ is the temple not "made with hands."[12] It is spiritual and incorporeal. Do not try to use Spirit to help matter. Do not try to use

~166~

Spirit to increase your matter. Do not try to use Spirit to decrease your matter. Do not try to use Spirit to destroy your enemies. Do not try to *use* Spirit!

The Christ is incorporeal, spiritual being, and Its embodiment is wholly spiritual, and therefore, your demonstration must be wholly spiritual. There is no use trying to confine It in a human body, a human group, or a human world. It will break the confines and spread the "remnants" all over the land. Christ is God, individually appearing as your being. Do not try to bottle It up as a body of flesh, or as a dollar bill. Rather, let the Christ manifest Itself as spiritual demonstration, and interpret Itself in terms of human experience. Do not let *you* do the interpreting! Let *It* do the interpreting. Learn this: There is not a problem you or I have, or ever have had, that did not come from trying to take Spirit and do something with It in the material realm.

If you are going to live a spiritual life in the spiritual realm, then let It translate Itself into terms of human good—companionship if It will. And if It does not so translate Itself, then be content to be alone with God. You are still in good company. Do not say to your friends, or even to yourself, "I am all alone. I have no friends." In that way you make yourself devoid of God, and if you are devoid of God, you *are* alone and without friends—and always will be.

When you keep your demonstration on the level of Spirit, of seeking first the kingdom of God and Its righteousness, It will interpret Itself in terms that you and I can understand in our daily existence. It will appear to us as friend, companion, husband, wife, or home. If we will only stop taking thought, stop trying to make It appear in some particular way, stop trying to bottle up Spirit in a finite body, home, or church! If we will keep our demonstration of Christ on the spiritual level, we immediately can come together as human beings for our common good. Do not try to take the Christ and personalize It as friend, husband, wife, or patient. You will not succeed. It will only give you more pain than pleasure. Let the Christ interpret Itself to you. Keep your demonstration on the spiritual level and do not try to visualize its outline, form, or expression. You will only have Paul and his churches, all over again.

Every time we come down below the level of our own understanding, lower than our own demonstrated state of consciousness, we condemn ourselves for it. Every time we live on a level of integrity lower than what we know to be our own integrity, we are uncomfortable; we do not like to look ourselves in the face.

Worse than that, however, is trying to use the Christ for material demonstration. That is the greatest sin there is against the Holy Ghost, and that is what destroys us. If we can only be content to keep our demonstration on the level of Spirit, and let Spirit Itself, in the spiritual tongue, translate Itself into the terms of our daily needs, we shall find that what appears to us as husband, wife, or companion will not fail us. Only human beings fail themselves and one another.

Freedom in Christ

If you understand that God has revealed Itself as your individual consciousness, that God has manifested Itself as your individual being, and if you are endeavoring to live up to what your idea of God and the Christ is, how then can you bring your thoughts down to terms of body, flesh, dollars, or houses and lots? The only way we can be free in Christ is to keep our demonstration on the spiritual level, and not try to bring it down to terms of finiteness, not try to use Spirit to function in a material concept or belief.

Since you accept yourself as the Christ of God, then accept yourself as incorporeal, not as having organs and functions, but as having the body "not made with hands, eternal in the heavens."[13] In the same way, since you are going to function as the individual Son of God, the infinite and invisible Son of God, then act as though you were "joint-heirs with Christ,"[14] and not as if you had to worry and scheme and plan how you were going to make a living. Try to live up to that highest sense of what you have understood to be your own identity. Do not try, in your treatment, to say, "I am the Christ of God," in one breath, and then continue with, "How about my rent?"

That is taking this spiritual Christ and trying to pin it down into a material demonstration. Let It manifest Itself, and It will manifest Itself in your consciousness in infinite demonstration—a demonstration not limited to this month's rent. It will manifest in supply unto eternity, for "Lo, I am with you alway, even unto the end of the world,"[15]—unto the end of all limitation, the end of all finiteness and corporeality—"I am with you until you have completely ascended in consciousness, ascended into the understanding of heaven on earth, of heaven here and now."

Paul had many troubles on his travels, but always Paul's troubles came about because he was taking this tremendous spiritual truth and trying either to jam it down someone's throat or to make some community come up to his ideal and his idea of spiritual living, usually a community not yet ready to live out from the spiritual sense of existence. It would be as if I were to say, "You must conform to my idea of life, if you want to study this truth." That is what Paul did and that was how he brought trouble upon himself. That is the way in which any one of us would get into trouble.

Oneness cannot be forced. Oneness is not the combining of people's thoughts and trying to make them all live up to some prescribed standard set by one person. Oneness comes only when each one is free in Spirit, when each one can live his own life to meet his highest ideal, with no one trying to be a reformer, or to set the standard for a home or a community. Each one must work out his own salvation and be guided by the Christ of his own being. I might say to you, "You must stop smoking," and perhaps you would. But it would not be a spiritual healing. At best, it would be a form of "human goodness," and some day you would have to meet that problem all over again.

Is it not better to reveal to you the infinite spiritual nature of your own being, and let that truth do the healing work? Why should anyone set himself up as a judge? Each has to come into this spiritual awareness in his own time, in his own way. Some of us need trouble to bring us in, others do not.

Miracles take place when the Christ touches consciousness. A human being cannot perform miracles, even if that human being is Jesus Christ! Only the Father within can reach out and touch consciousness, open it, and make it realize it is one with God, make it realize its oneness with God. Christ never was, and never will be mortal. Christ is the Son of God appearing as that which we call man. Do you believe on him whom the Father has sent? Who was *I Am?* Who is *I Am?* None but you! God sent Himself forth into manifestation, as you. At one period you think yourself bad, at another, good, or sick, or well; until you realize this truth, and then you say:

I am not a human being! I never was a human being! I am the Christ of God made manifest! God, Himself, goes forth into expression as the Son of God. None of the trials and tribulations or sins of the present, past, or future, can ever attach themselves to that which I am. God, Himself, went forth as the Son into the world, to manifest the Christ of God, to show forth the mind that was in Christ Jesus, to show forth the Spirit, Soul, and body of God. I am the very body of God, the temple of the living God, the temple of the Holy Ghost—the very presence of God, Itself, made manifest as individual being.

~ 10 ~

THE MINISTRY OF THE CHRIST

We should never undertake anything, even so unimportant a thing as going to the corner for a loaf of bread, without first making our conscious contact with God. The reason is that while we may seem to be out only for the purpose of buying a loaf of bread, we, actually, may be out on some God-mission without knowing it. If we have not made our contact, we may never know what that mission was and so fail to recognize an opportunity to lend ourselves consciously to this work.

Nothing is ever what it appears to be in the human picture. We often think that we are doing something for a normal, natural, human reason and, later on, find that this was not at all the real purpose of what we did. The human reason is sometimes only the decoy that sends us on the real mission, and the true purpose was perhaps not apparent to us at all.

We should know by now that as human beings, we are only a transparency for the Divine. Actually, our purpose in studying spiritual wisdom is to find out, through meditation, what the spiritual plan is, and what our part in it is. As we make our contact, we become the visible transparency for the inner, divine, spiritual plan. Then, God, infinite Spirit, is able to use us and to manifest Itself as our individual being, working out Its plan on what we humanly call the earth.

It is the earth, but it is more than just the earth: It is both heaven *and* earth. Heaven and earth are not two different and separate places, except in the human sense of time and place. Reality knows no such thing as "time," no such thing as "place." Time is really *now;* place is *here.* Whether or not this earth is a hell or a heaven is dependent upon your view of it, because where some find heaven, others find hell. Some of us find enjoyment in many places right here on earth; others find suffering in the very same places. It is all in the point of view, in the attitude of the individual. Heaven is not a place, and hell is not a place. They are states of consciousness, here and now.

There is only one way to find your heaven on earth, and that is through inner contact with God. Rest assured that all that humanhood is, is a sense of separation from God. All that divine being is, is conscious oneness with God. In the purely personal, almost mechanical process of getting up in the morning, going out to your daily work, and then going back to bed again at night, you are a human being, subject to all the experiences of humanhood, which include temptation, disease, lack, worry, and danger. But, in making contact with God so that you feel it, so that you actually catch that sense of awareness, you let your humanhood become the transparency through which the Divinity of you is shining. Then, you are no longer living your own life; God is living Its life *as* you.

In metaphysics, we say, "God is mind." We even say, "God is my mind." And then we try to go on having a human will of our own, without consulting this mind of God as to Its idea, will, or plan. We do not give It an opportunity to function, but we, ourselves, go out and do what we think is right for that day. In the same way, we declare, "God is life," usually adding, "God is my life." Yet we turn around and feel sad or worried. About what? About our life—the life which we have just stated is God? Over and over again we declare that God is divine love. We go a step further and say, "God is the very love of my being." Yet, we do not hesitate to criticize, judge, condemn, hate, and fear each other.

As human beings, all this may be permissible. As human beings, perhaps, we all have the right to do what we will with our life. But we, who have taken this path, have no such rights. We have absolutely no right to wear the robe of the Christ, and not take on the full responsibilities that come with the wearing of it. Every one coming into a spiritual teaching is, in a measure, taking on the Robe, not only as a practitioner, but also as a teacher. This is true of every individual who is claiming some degree of Christ-guidance in his life. The Robe is a symbolic term for the assumption of Christ qualities.

Anyone taking on a measure of Christhood, turning to the Christ for healing, for supply, for direction —anyone who has in any degree taken on the robe of Christ—must acknowledge that there is no use being disturbed, and no use complaining, if the Christ does not function. We know that we may fail, but that the Christ never fails. If there is failure, we must acknowledge that we are not making the contact with the Christ; we are not making the specific contact through meditation.

Contact with God

The purpose of meditation is not to think a lot of thoughts and declare truths. Its real object is direct contact with God. No one but a child would play with an instrument as useful as the telephone. We adults pick it up for the specific purpose of making contact with someone, somewhere. In this work, too, we have a specific contact to make—a specific number to reach, G-o-d! There is no way to achieve the guidance and direction of God except by tuning in and listening for, and ultimately hearing the "still small voice," which does not necessarily mean hearing audibly, although it sometimes comes that way.

We mean receiving the sense, awareness, or feeling of that Presence. Why make statements such as, "God is directing and protecting me," and continue to experience accidents, sin, disease, and death? The statement, "God is with me," is no insurance policy. Not all the affirmations in the world that "God is with me," or "God is presence; God is power; God is my life," can save us, because these statements are merely steps on the way. The only time that we, actually, know that God is omnipresent and omnipotent and omniscient—on the job—is when we have made the contact, and know that we have made it, or at least, have opened our consciousness to make it. There are times when we open our consciousness and do not receive a direct answer or have the feeling that we have succeeded in making the contact. But that is not too important. The important thing is to have opened consciousness to the contact, to have sat down even for a moment and to have said, "Father, here I am. Be with me."

In this way we have opened our consciousness to the inflow. We have fulfilled Scripture: "Thou wilt keep him in perfect peace, whose mind is stayed on thee[1] . . . Lean not unto thine own understanding. In all thy ways acknowledge him."[2] We can all remember to stop to listen, while we go about our housekeeping, buying, or business. "Lean not unto thine own understanding." Do not lean even on your own hearing ability, or on trying to understand rationally the meaning of what you hear or read. Lean on your spiritual understanding and spiritual wisdom, on that mind that was in Christ Jesus, which was and is your mind. Lean on that to interpret to you what you read and what you hear.

Take any one of these wonderful quotations that we have been reading in the Bible, and not obeying. "The Lord will perfect that which concerneth me."[3] Does He? Has He? Look over your human life and see whether He really has made all that concerns you perfect. In most cases, you will find that He has not, and the reason He has not is because you have not opened your conscious-ness to let Him in. God is omnipotence, certainly. But what good is that to you, unless *you* open your con-sciousness specifically and make yourself a transparency for It, or for Him, to enter in?

If you could follow scriptural history about the time of Jesus, you would know how many hundreds of thousands of people never were aware of the birth of the Christ, never acknowledged it, or even wondered if there weren't a fire somewhere! No, they did not even smell the "smoke." The birth of the Christ could have raised the entire Hebrew people up into the highest state of spiritual realization. But how many Hebrews received or accepted the Christ? So few that another religion developed, based entirely upon the one who had been rejected of his own people. "He came unto his own, and his own received him not."[4]

The fact that the Christ was before Abraham and will be unto the end of the world is no assurance to you that

It is going to do anything for you. It is true, "Before Abraham was, I am,"[5] and "I am with you alway, even unto the end of the world."[6] With whom? Only with those who open their consciousness to It! Only with those who become receptive, those who learn to listen for the "still small voice."[7]

Dedication

The experience of entertaining the Christ, of living by the Christ, comes only to those who actually make the contact, who actually feel the divine Presence, and who know consciously that It is moving them about from here to there. In our humanhood and by our human actions we never know the real purpose behind those actions. If we are in tune with the Infinite, the Divine has a way of using us to Its purpose—not to glorify us or to show forth what good demonstrators of truth we are, not to show how great a practice, or income, or position, we can attain. Its purpose has nothing to do with that. Its use of us must, in some way, show forth God's works. Let God's plan be revealed in you, but never have your heart so set on a demonstration that you are not equally satisfied to see it turn out otherwise—"not my will, but thine, be done."[8]

Do you not see the necessity for keeping your consciousness open to God's direction? Otherwise, we would be going along in the same old path we have been on for years and years. Why was it that we changed? *We* didn't. What happened was that, in some measure, our consciousness was opened to divine direction, probably because we were willing to set aside stated periods every day and every night for tuning in, for opening consciousness, for saying, "Father, walk in and take over." We were preparing for that dedication and consecration which would enable us to say, truly, "I live, yet not I, but Christ liveth in me."[9] Then, every day we rededicate ourselves: "Father, here I am. My mind, my Soul, my body—all are yours. You take them. You take over." Unless we do dedicate and consecrate ourselves, we shall never live more than a human existence which begins at birth and ends in the grave. If we do adopt and open consciousness to this method of living, we soon shall find that we are not living a human life after all. Truth, Life, Soul, Intelligence—all really are God; yes, even the body is the temple of the living God. We shall find, then, that God is using all there is of us to Its purpose.

The main goal in our earlier study of metaphysics was to find some system whereby we could increase our health, happiness, and prosperity. But this is a different stage of development, a higher state of development in which we now say: "Father, I do not care about my life, or my pocketbook. You use me. Make me a part of the divine plan. Let me fit in where I belong in the spiritual picture." That is our present state of consciousness, if we are truly dedicated and consecrated. It is letting God use our eyes, our feet, our body, our Soul, our mind, for Its purpose.

Who is to say that there need ever be another war? Why should these horrors continue? Only because the world is full of human beings living their own lives, each intent upon improving his own pocketbook. We cannot condemn them for this self-seeking; we cannot criticize them: They have not yet come into spiritual unfoldment. But *we* can be blamed, if from this point on, we act in any such way. Can we really have a purpose of our own now? Can we continue to be dedicated to our own little personal selfhood, or to parents, wife, husband, or children, exclusively? How can we say that God is revealing Itself as our life, our mind, and our body, and yet have the audacity to use that infinite Power, that infinite Presence, only to patch up our own little human affairs? Are we not aware of the great truth of the infinite nature of our own being—of the infinite nature—the spiritual nature of our mind and Soul and consciousness—so that we are willing to dedicate ourselves and let ourselves be used from this time forth as a focal point for the unfoldment of the divine plan?

The Purpose of the Christ Ministry

The Christ ministry reveals the nature of God as individual consciousness. This ministry is a constant realization of God as individual consciousness, as your consciousness and mine, and the consciousness of all the people we meet. Then, even though we shall ultimately rise above the human desire to help people, our realization of their true identity will be of immeasurable help, because God, as their consciousness, is capable of giving them all the help they require. The help they really need is to have one person—only one—recognize that God is their consciousness. They are believing that all they have is a human mortality which is just not equal to the burdens of the world. Therefore, as we walk up and down this world, without any sense of desiring to help anyone, let us rejoice within our own being that, since God is the unfolded, revealed, and expressed consciousness of individual being, each one contains within himself the entire Christ, and that is all that is necessary for his fulfilment.

That is the purpose of the ministry as it interprets Itself to us. People function in this ministry in many capacities—as physicians, lawyers, legislators, teachers, businessmen, homemakers. All these activities can fulfil the scriptural injunction to "love thy neighbor as thyself,"[10] and to "love the Lord thy God with all thy heart, and with all thy soul, and with all thy mind."[11] That love, as you so well know, has degrees and gradations. At one point in our experience, the highest that was expected of us was that we make a contribution to a community fund, or a sanatorium, or a children's home. Today we are still asked to do those things, and we are doing them as a part of loving our neighbor as ourselves, on his level of consciousness. That, however, is not our Christ ministry. The work which has been given us to do in the Infinite Way is to live in the conscious realization of God, unfolding, revealing, and disclosing Itself as individual consciousness.

Then, what happens? God, the mind of the individual, is all the power in the world to that individual. The mind of the individual, then, becomes a focal point through which and as which God acts for the good of the individual. Wherever you are and whatever you do, remember that your function is so to live as to realize consciously that God is the life and the Soul and the mind and the consciousness of individual being. Individual being is empowered with all that God is: "Son, thou art ever with me, and all that I have is thine . . ."[12] If you make your bed in hell, there am I."

As we live consciously in this consciousness, we bless others. That is the method that has been given to us for blessing the world, or that part of it which comes within range of our consciousness. That is our particular function and our particular method of working. Did you ever stop to think that there is a spiritual underground, that throughout the world there are people praying daily in the way we have been taught to pray? These people form this spiritual underground, and each one is praying in accordance with the highest light that has been given to him, the highest light he is capable of receiving at this moment. So likewise, is it given to us to be a spiritual underground, to be silent workers, to be silent pray-ers.

"Love the Lord, thy God . . ." but do not forget the second half of the commandment: "Love thy neighbor as thyself." That neighbor, as we have brought out so often, is really every individual on earth. In *Conscious Union with God,*[*] this theme was developed: "My conscious oneness with God constitutes my oneness with all spiritual being and idea." Because of that contact, all the good that is flowing to us, will, through our oneness with all, flow outward. Because of that truth, all the good of God flows to us through every spiritual being. We are a channel, an underground, a wire system through which the good of God flows from others to us, and through us out to others. All that God has and all that God is, is flowing through me to all in the universe, and through all in the universe to me.

Now let us realize God as individual consciousness —the infinity of God appearing as individuals. Let us accept that message and that mission. Let us accept the consecration and dedication it requires, and let us determine that, in so far as it is given to us to do, we will fulfill our mission as part of God's plan. And then see what happens to us!

---

*By the author.

But let us not in any way confuse the idea of spiritual unfoldment with material demonstration, nor expect that through thinking "right" thoughts or "spiritual" thoughts, we can buy a material demonstration or gain the power to demonstrate material things. Keep your demonstration in the realm of Spirit. When you turn to Spirit for help, desire only spiritual good. We are living in a higher state of unfoldment than that of demonstrating things and persons. When we turn to God, let us pray for "the things of God." Ninety percent of our failure to experience harmony is that we are turning to Spirit for material demonstration. We only have the right to turn to God for the "things of God," and then let God interpret those things to us. Let the Christ interpret the things of God in terms of what appear to us as human needs.

The question frequently is raised: Whom shall we heal? To whom shall we respond when there is a request for help? To whom shall we deny help? Should it make any difference to us whether the one reaching out for help is a Jew, a Catholic, or a Protestant? Should we ask if he is in a hospital, in a prison, or a member of a metaphysical organization? Insofar as we are concerned, we have the presence of God before us in that very person asking for help—God appearing as the mind and consciousness of individual being. That is the truth. That is what we are called upon to know, regardless of who asks for help—or what, or why, or when.

Let not that which God created ever appear in our sight as unholy or unclean. We are not dealing with a mortal concept of man; we are dealing with God's creation. We are not knowing the truth about "man, whose breath is in his nostrils."[13] Rather have we been told to "take no thought for man, whose breath is in his

~183~

nostrils." When a call comes to us, there must be the instant recognition that this is "the mind that was in Christ Jesus." That is our message—the recognition of God appearing as individual being.

In the human course of events, we who stand for this principle or message will meet with criticism, judgement, and condemnation, depending upon the viewpoint of the one who is examining our mission and our message. Let us be wise. Let us be very wise. Our work, our message, and our mission need no defense. Let none of us ever, at any time, be found defending this message. It would be wise to maintain that attitude, regardless of what message you are following or what mission. Never defend it. Let its fruit bear witness to it. Those who find fault with our particular approach, may very honestly misunderstand our message and our mission. In that case, it becomes necessary only to say, "Read the books; judge for yourself; and then follow or not, as you will." It is possible that personal sense will enter into criticism and condemnation and judgement of us, and in that case any defense would be a waste of time. You cannot convince anyone against his own will, and again we say, "Read for yourself."

Make this message your own individual demonstration. Always remember that never are you called upon to defend this message or your connection with it. Let the message be judged by its fruits and let its intent and purpose be shown forth by the Writings. If the Writings do not explain and clarify themselves, nothing you can add will clarify them.

You have been given the teaching that God appears as individual you and me, the message that God appears, unfolds, and discloses Himself as the life and consciousness of individual being. So never, in your thought, accept anyone on the earth as other than the manifestation of God's own selfhood.

Franz Kafka has told us that we need not do much about anything except to stand still—and not even stand still. Just sit quietly—and not even sit quietly. His words were: "You do not need to leave your room. Remain sitting at your table, and listen. Do not even listen, simply wait. Do not even wait, be quite still and solitary. The world will freely offer itself to you to be unmasked, it has no choice, it will roll in ecstasy at your feet."*

This comes very near to being the highest unfoldment we shall ever receive in the way of making what we call our "demonstration." Since the mind of us, the individual consciousness of us, is God, is there anything that I can possibly have that you need, which is not being disclosed to you at all times? Less and less of human effort is required when more and more of God is revealed as our individual mind. Much less has to be said between us to bring about understanding, when God is understood to be not only the mind of you and of me, but of every individual on earth. Others may not consciously understand how God can be their mind, but your knowing it and my knowing it brings us together in richer fellowship. It brings us into oneness with every individual on earth with whom there is any necessity for contact.

There are two important points to be considered seriously in this ministry: One is this realization of God as your mind and life, which we have been discussing.

---

*Franz Kafka, *Great Wall of China, Series and Reflections,* trans. Willa and Edwin Muir (New York: Schocken Books, 1946), p. 307.

The second is the acceptance of the meaning involved in the word "now." In this work, we are learning to make a conscious effort to live now—not yesterday, and not tomorrow—but now. If we can learn to live as if this moment were life eternal and if, in this moment, we can realize that God is manifesting Its will in us and through us; life will be a continuous now; even tomorrow will be now, and twenty years hence and a hundred years hence will be now. There can be no aging when we learn to live in this infinite moment. In this moment, if God is our life, what have we to fear of life in this moment? All that is necessary is the continuous realization of this now-ness!

It is in this moment of now that God is acting as the universal consciousness. It is in this very moment of now that God is expressing the infinity of Its intelligence and life and love throughout the spiritual universe. All that we are told to do is to abide in this now. "Now are we the sons of God"[14]—not will be. Now is God manifesting Its glory as my individual being. Now am I the son of God. Now is God manifesting Its glory as the individual being of all mankind. Now is God manifesting the peace "which passeth all understanding."[15] All that we have to do is to abide in this now and not worry about what is going to take place tomorrow or be concerned for what happened yesterday. Yesterday can never appear again, and tomorrow can never arrive because there is only now. Whatever time there is, is now; there is, there can only be now. And what is the truth about now? The allness of God made manifest as individual being is all that is taking place now!

If you can accept God manifested as your individual being *now* and then just leave it at that, you will find how quickly the errors of sense slough off. They disappear by themselves in a miracle of light. However, more often than not, there is a gradual dropping away of the errors. But either gradual or instantaneous, a dropping away of the error can come about only in the consciousness of now. It can come about only in the consciousness that now God is. Now is the infinity of God manifesting Its glory as individual being, yours and mine.

We can think of God as intelligence and realize that the divine Intelligence, the infinite, spiritual Wisdom, is manifesting Its eternal glory as the intelligence of you and of me and of all mankind. We can do the same thing with all the synonyms for God, realizing that at this very moment the infinity of the Godhead is made manifest as the life, truth, love, intelligence, Spirit, Soul, principle, cause, and effect of this entire universe. In this way, we bring together all the work, all the unfoldment, we have had and cement it together in these two ideas:

1. The infinity of God appears as individual being.

2. God, in the infinity of Its being, unfolds and reveals Itself, here and now—eternally here and now.

~ 11 ~

GRATITUDE

Only those who understand that God is their own consciousness and that from this individual, yet infinite, consciousness flow all things can really know the true sense of gratitude. The only real gratitude is that which is felt for the gift of spiritual discernment. All else is but thankfulness for things.

Three times or more, Jesus fed the multitudes. He fed four thousand, five thousand, seven thousand. Today we would call that an act of great philanthropy. Not only did he feed the multitudes, but he healed them and taught the truth to those who could hear. But after he had fed the multitudes on one side of the sea, he felt a heavy sense within himself—a sense that his message had not reached his people, a sense of discouragement in the realization that they had failed to catch the vision. We are told that he left them and went across the lake, but even there the multitudes followed him. Probably they followed him because they were hungry again and wanted more loaves and fishes. He must have recognized that loaves and fishes were all they wanted because he turned and rebuked them: "You are here because you received the loaves and fishes yesterday, and now you have come back for more of them. Why is it that you did not see the miracle? Why is it that you did not see the principle that produced those loaves and fishes, so that by now some of you could have been producing and multiplying loaves and fishes on your own, and not coming back to me to be fed?"

How often he healed the multitudes—how often he healed individuals—and how little healing power any of those people manifested themselves! How great was his sorrow when he said, "Jerusalem, Jerusalem, I would love to tell you and show you, but you cannot accept it." Those people whom he had healed and had supplied were grateful; they were grateful for the loaves and fishes. But that was not the type of gratitude the Master was seeking. The Master was seeking gratitude for a principle that he was showing forth and which they were not able to grasp. Their whole thought was on the *effect*, and not on the *cause*. The tragedy of the entire mission of Jesus was that so many were grateful for the effects, and so few caught the vision of the cause—few were able to go out and do likewise. In the ministry of the Master, there is a principle shown forth. It is a principle of living, a principle of healing, a principle of supply. As you read the New Testament, see if you cannot discern the principle he was trying to set forth and also notice that the people he helped saw only the effect of that principle.

Had Jesus been merely a wonder worker, had he desired merely to set himself up as a great man, a great teacher, a great healer, or a great supplier, he would not have had to undergo the Crucifixion. There would have been no necessity for it. He would have set up a clinic and branch clinics for healing people, and super-markets for supplying them, and just continued multiplying the goods in the markets, letting people come, partake, and be grateful. There would have been a deep gratitude in the hearts of those people, because they would no longer have had to till the soil, or operate meat markets, fish markets, and vegetable markets. How easy life would have been! All that would have been necessary would have been to go to the store where Jesus was multiplying loaves and fishes. Or how easy it would have been to go to the clinics where his disciples would have established themselves and would be saying: "Come on in and be healed! Without money and without price! Well, pay a little mite if you like, a little love offering, but come and get rid of all your diseases. We'll do it for you." Oh, the people would have been so grateful!

Be Grateful for the Principle

Yet Jesus never attempted that type of demonstration. Only three or four times in his whole ministry did he multiply loaves and fishes. Only a few times did he heal the multitudes. If you had noticed Jesus walking up and down by the shores of Galilee, you would not have found him looking around for sick people to heal. Usually, he passed right by them, but they ran after him, calling out, "Oh, Master, Master! Heal me!" Yes, his people were grateful for the loaves and fishes and would have continued to feel that sense of gratitude had he kept on giving them effects, effects, and more effects. But that sense of gratitude—a gratitude for effects—was not the type of gratitude for which he was looking. He was looking for the gratitude of those who could discern the principle behind the miracle. It is that same type of gratitude that we in this work are looking for today. It is not the gratitude that causes people to come and say, "Oh, that was a beautiful healing! Here is a check." We much prefer to hear: "That was a beautiful healing! How was it accomplished? What was the principle behind it? Teach me the principle."

In this work, it is a very easy thing to arouse gratitude in the hearts of people. We hear again and again: "Your writing is so inspiring. You bring out such spiritual stories and incidents. You draw on such a world of scriptural history and literature, and other inspirational, philosophical, and metaphysical literature!" It is not a difficult thing to arouse people to a state of gratitude. But the real teacher is not seeking that type of gratitude. It is well enough that people feel a gratitude for the message, but the real gratitude which makes the spiritual teacher rejoice is that which comes from those who are catching the vision and saying: "Thank you, I saw the Christ. Thank you, I have experienced the very presence of God, and now I can go out and do likewise, even if it is only in a measure!"

We are taught that the Pilgrim Fathers came to the New World to find religious freedom. There is nothing further from the truth than that. Our Pilgrim Fathers did not come here for religious freedom. They came to seek an opportunity to preach a religion of their own and to make everybody conform to it. The moment anybody dared to disagree with their religious practices, even though they, themselves, had been dissenters, he was forced out of the colony. There was little of religious freedom in those early days. Anyone who, like Roger Williams, would not conform to the established religion was exiled from the colony because the colonists would permit no deviation from their prescribed form of worship.

It is not in the nature of most people to want religious freedom. What they really want is the freedom to practice their own religion, and then to force it upon the rest of mankind. That was the Colonists' interpretation of religious liberty. At the first Thanksgiving, the Pilgrims gave thanks, not because they had found a land where they could practice religious freedom, but because they had found a land where they could practice their own particular form of religion. They gave thanks for an effect, for something in the visible realm. Had the gratitude of the Pilgrim Fathers been of the kind that we are being taught, it would have been for a principle of real freedom, a principle so universal, so impersonal, that they would have extended it equally to all men. Then their gratitude would have been for cause, for principle, for universal good. But it was not that kind of gratitude. It was for their own safety, their own security, and for the right to do as they pleased.

We, in the twentieth century, must examine our own attitude toward the giving of thanks. Instead of being grateful that we have a United States of America which is comparatively free, our gratitude should be for a sense of spiritual freedom which is God-given, and which can never be interfered with by "man, whose breath is in his nostrils," nor by any form of government that he may devise. Governments change; administrations come and go; and if our gratitude rests on a satisfaction in these forms and only in the forms, we may find ourselves rudely awakened. The forms can too easily shift from our concept of good to our concept of evil. Therefore, instead of being grateful for the *effect*–some human form of government–we, on the spiritual path, have learned that our gratitude should be for a *principle* of government, and for the fact that we have discovered enough about the principle to maintain it and sustain it in individual and collective consciousness so that no man or group of men can tear it down. When we learn this, we shall have learned a higher sense of gratitude.

It is the same with healing. Instead of being grateful for a physical healing or grateful that your income has been doubled through a practitioner's work or grateful that business is better, be grateful that there is a principle that will do these things for you, and that the principle is available to you: Turn your thanks and gratitude into gaining a realization of the principle that is involved.

There was a time when it was thought that only "masters" had access to this principle. One had to be a priest, a rabbi, or a minister in order to know this great principle of healing. Then, everyone else would come along and say, "Oh, how wonderful you are! Please do me this great favor!" Today, this principle of life, which includes the principle of healing and the principle of multiplying loaves and fishes, is available to you and to me. Nobody has a monopoly on it. Even the copyrights on our Infinite Way books are only for the particular words used in presenting this principle. But that same principle can be stated in your own words for which you, too, can secure a copyright. Nobody can copyright or patent the idea of spiritual healing, or the idea of multiplying loaves and fishes. It is an open secret, and it is available to everybody. Our gratitude today should be that this principle is available, that it is known, and that it can be practiced.

Certainly, there are loaves and fishes connected with this work. You, as an individual, must go within your own being, and pray and pray and pray for the Father within to reveal to you your teacher and your teaching. You will not be misled if you go within. Pray; pray; pray within your own being! Turn to the Father within and say: "Show me my teacher! Show me my teaching!" Then, when you are led to some teaching, stay with it—and not just because you have a healing. It is good to be grateful. There is nothing finer than a sense of gratitude for the work that someone has done for you, especially when it has borne fruit. But there is something higher. Do not be satisfied. Turn within; go deeper. If you have received help, ask, "You have worked this miracle! Now tell me how you did it. Show me. Teach me." And if there is a spiritual spark in you, it will not be too long before you will be performing the same miracles.

If it is difficult and takes longer than you anticipated, be patient. It is not given to everyone to grasp this spiritual idea quickly. If you have a well-developed intellect, you may learn the letter of it very quickly and then be disappointed when it does not work. So you may complain, "I know all there is to be known, but I do not get the healing!" In that case, you have not gone far enough. You have to go deep enough until you reach that point where your heart is touched, where your Spirit is quickened, where the Christ comes to life. That is not accomplished through mere intellectual attainment.

There are others of you who may not grasp it so quickly, intellectually, but do not be disturbed about that, either. Much of this work is done without knowing how it is done. The Christ touches consciousness, and the Christ does the work.

In either case, be patient! Let your heart tell you when you have found your teacher, and then be patient! Stay on the path, and catch the vision of this principle.

Then you will have fulfilled the mission that Jesus came to earth to prove. He did not come to earth to multiply loaves and fishes for the poverty-stricken people of the world. He did not come to earth to be a doctor for humanity. Jesus came to earth to reveal the principle of the Christ. If you are satisfied with anything less than that principle, you are not really interested in the Christ-mission.

There is not a teacher of spiritual wisdom or a practitioner whom the Christ has touched who is satisfied merely to multiply loaves and fishes for you, or to heal your body. His only aim and desire is to do that for you in order to show you that this is the principle, and that this is the way. You remember, do you not, that when John, the Baptist, was in prison and no one came to rescue him, he began to doubt as to whether or not Jesus was the Christ? For years he had gone up and down the countryside telling the people about Jesus. Now, here he was in a dungeon and had not been shown the way out. He sent word to Jesus. Do you remember Jesus' great answer: "Go and shew John again those things which ye do hear and see: The blind receive their sight, and the lame walk, the lepers are cleansed, and the deaf hear, the dead are raised up and the poor have the gospel preached to them."[1] That is the Christ ministry. You notice that he did not say: "Yes, I am authorized. Here is my diploma." His answer was: "The sick are healed!"

That is the answer. When your ills of body or mind or morals or purse are being healed—when your consciousness is being lifted into a higher sense of life than the material one—then, whoever is doing that for you is showing you the principle, or he could not be doing it.

No teacher or practitioner wants to be engaged on a permanent monthly basis to do spiritual healing work for you. What he wants is for you to say, "Please, show me the way." Then, from there on, *it is up to you.*

I have never known of a teacher on this path who has been touched by the Christ, who was not eager to teach this principle to any one and every one reaching out for it. A teacher becomes weary only of those who keep coming to him, saying, "Well, yesterday it was the left corn; now it is the right knee; and oh, that left hip!" We practitioners love the healing work. We never outgrow our love for it. But we love it only for one reason and that is because sometimes it leads our patients to say, "Yes, I had a healing. Tell me, how was it done?"

If by chance any one of us should develop into the ablest healer in the world, do you realize that in his entire human span he could not heal very many people? It would be only a drop in the bucket, those few hundred or few thousand, or even few tens of thousands that he could heal. But, if one individual could be responsible for even three others going out into the world and doing what I am doing, or what you may be doing, we would have multiplied our usefulness threefold in the doing, in fact, more than threefold, because each one of those in his turn might find three more to send forth to do likewise. Do you see what that one little drop of Christ consciousness would be doing out in the world? Through multiplication?

It is the same with every spiritual teacher. It is the same with every spiritual practitioner. It makes no difference whose banner we are under, or whether we are under any banner at all except the Christ Itself. The point is that if everyone who can do a little healing work would teach just one other person to do healing work, in a very few generations, the world would no more find a cause for war than you or I would have cause for quarreling with one another. The Spirit wipes any desire for fighting out of us. It erases all intolerance, injustice, or any lurking sense of dishonesty or sensuality.

In other words, that Spirit which is loosed in those of us who gather for no other purpose than for the unveiling of the Christ, for no other purpose than for learning the true meaning of gratitude—that Spirit alone would change, not only our own lives and bodies, but our relationship with tradespeople, with employers, and with employees. The whole life of our community would be transformed.

Summary of the Letter of Truth

Somebody may say, "This is a beautiful idea, but would I be capable of doing this? Is it given to me to be able to do this?" Why not? God is no respecter of persons, and the letter of truth is a very simple thing to master. In less than five minutes, you can learn all the letter of truth that has ever been written in any bible of the world. From there on, it is not a question of whether or not you know enough truth, but whether or not you *love this life*—whether you love this purpose enough to live it and to go out and demonstrate it.

To show you how simple it is to know the truth that makes you free, I shall sum it up very, very briefly for you. Remember that Jesus said: "Know the truth, and the truth shall make you free."[2] He did not say, "The truth will make you free." He said, *"Know* the truth, and the truth shall make you free."

What is the truth that we are supposed to know? In the first place, it consists of knowing what God is. Everyone must know what God is. If you do not know what God is, you are not even on the first step of the way. How do you learn what God is? From the revelation of Jesus Christ, and from those who are expounding the principle of the Christ. If you turn back to Jesus Christ, you will find that he said, "I am life eternal." Did you ever stop to think of the meaning of that statement? What difference does it make whether or not I am sick or well, if I am going to live forever? It takes the fear right out of disease. "I am life eternal!"—not, "I will be eternal, *if* I learn some truth." You do not have to learn any truth. You are already life eternal, and that is the only truth you have to learn. "I am truth; I am Spirit; I am Soul; I am divine." The Master said, "Hast thou not known me, Philip? he that hath seen me hath seen the Father . . .³ I and my Father are one."⁴ You do not have to wonder any more what God is:

God is the intelligence of the universe; God is the infinite life of the universe, whether that universe is you, the plants, the trees, the animals, the birds, or the insects. God is the life of all being. God is the intelligence, the divine love, the infinite wisdom of all being.

All that God is, I am; all that the Father hath is mine. I do not have to seek for it; I do not even have to get it. I and the Father are one: I contain it.

Isn't that a miracle! You do not have to be concerned about demonstrating anything after tonight. You do not have to take thought, or give yourself a treatment for supply. From now on, your treatment is: "I and the

Father are one, and all that the Father hath is mine!" How can that law be changed? That law was laid down long before Jesus' time. Jesus is just the exponent of it for the Western world. It is a law that existed before the time of Jesus, and he himself admitted this when he said: "Before Abraham was, I am."[5] Before Abraham was, this truth is. He also said: "I am with you alway, even unto the end of the world."[6] This truth which existed before Abraham, this truth is going to be with you until the end of the world. What truth? *This* truth:

I and the Father are one, and all that the Father is, I am. Son, all that I have is thine. The place whereon I stand is holy ground, and if I make my bed in hell, lo, I am there. Why? Because this is not just God; this is I and the Father; and I and the Father are one. Wherever I am, God is. We are one. Wherever God is, I am. And wherever God is, all that the Father hath, is. The eternal life of the Father is my eternal life; the immortality of God is the immortality of my being.

The immortality of God is the immortality of my body, since my body is the "temple of the living God," since God is the substance of which my body is formed. God is the infinite substance of the universe, divine Spirit, of which this universe is formed and even of my body which is as immortal as my life, or my mind.

You cannot separate your life or your mind except in belief, and when you do that, there is a funeral. But you bring about that funeral by accepting the world-belief in a separation between God and God's creation. Since God is the consciousness of you, and since that consciousness is unfolding and revealing Itself as *form*—which we call creation—you cannot separate God from Its creation.

That is why the sun and the stars and the moon keep going on and on and on. Nobody believes that you can separate God from the sun, moon, and stars. People only believe that you can separate God from your body. Get over any such belief! Remember:

I and the Father are one. God is the substance and the intelligence of this universe, and that means God is the substance and the intelligence of my being and my body. My body is the temple of the living God, and God is flowing through it. All that the Father hath, is mine—not to be demonstrated, not to be achieved, but mine now, because of my relationship of sonship.

Notice that you do not even have to be what is called a good person. Do not condemn yourself. Realize that it was your ignorance that led you into whatever error you may have been guilty of indulging. That same ignorance led you into the belief that your body was something apart from God, and that you could do what you wanted to do with it. No, that you can never do: Your body is the temple of the living God and you must treat it as if it were of God, and let it show forth the glory that is God.

In these two points are contained two-thirds of the letter of truth. The last third deals with the reason that we have sin, disease, lack and limitation. Somewhere, sometime, the belief in a selfhood apart from God sprang up. In biblical literature, it is illustrated in the story of the prodigal son, who wandered away from his father's house and set up an identity of his own. It was not long before he found that the separate identity was not sufficient to maintain and to sustain him. When he awakened to his true identity, he returned to his father,

"Here, you take over, Father; be the mind of me, and the life of me."

Somewhere in history, the human race, or what we now know as the human race, wandered off and away from the Father consciousness, and decided, "I can make a living for myself; I want to be an independent being; I would like to do with my own life what I choose to do with it for a change." That set up an identity apart from God, and from that minute on we have had to "work for a living." We have had to work to support our body, home, business, and community. Yet all we have to do is to realize:

Father, all Your wealth is mine; all Your life is my life; all the intelligence of You is the intelligence of me; and I am a witness to all Thou art. I am that place in consciousness through which You can manifest and express.

The minute you realize this, you are aware that all error is merely the belief that you are an identity by yourself, something separate and apart from God, and that you have a life to support, a body to feed, and a house and clothes to maintain. But all that is an illusion. The truth is that your life and your body are for God to maintain and sustain. You have been taking that prerogative away from God and setting yourself up as something apart from God.

An actor on the stage sometimes plays the part of a beggar, for which he may be paid five thousand dollars a week. But how unfortunate it would be for him, if he really believed himself to be the character he was playing and thereby separated himself from his five thousand dollar weekly salary! How ridiculous it would be for him to believe that he was a beggar, just because he was acting that part in a play. But that is what we have done in this human experience: We have set up our own identity; we have called ourselves "beggars"; we have believed ourselves not fit to sit at the feet of the Master. People forget that these human experiences are parts which they are playing in a drama of ignorance. In reality, the very one who is playing it, is the child of God, the offspring of God—God manifested. In fact, he is God's own being Itself in individual form and expression.

Will you believe me when I tell you that this is all there is to be known of truth? I do not care how many books I have written about it and shall continue to write; that is all I have ever said in any of them, so far as the letter of truth is concerned. I may have gone a step further and pointed out that what has just been said constitutes treatment, and then have gone another step to emphasize that inasmuch as this is only the letter of truth it is not enough. After you have stated the truth, affirmed and reaffirmed it in your own consciousness, sit back and wait for the "still small voice" to confirm it, to give it the "click"; and then your demonstration is complete.

This is the truth of being. Of itself, however, it will not be enough to enable you to heal or to be healed. One step more is necessary and that is the spiritual awareness of this truth. That, you cannot get from a man, from a woman, or from a book. That, you have to get from the Father within you.

After I have told you this truth and after you understand it, there may be enough of the fire of the Christ in my consciousness to set you free from some particular discord at this moment. There have been enough testimonies of healings that have taken place to know that this is true. My thirty-two years in this work and my great love for it have engendered enough of the divine spark in me so that some are lifted up and experience healing. That is an effect of my consciousness, but you yourself do not have the principle, until you can bring it forth as healing.

Be Grateful that You Have Touched The Christ

The letter of truth is the foundation upon which all of your treating is done. You can, from this simple truth, build for yourself hours and hours and hours of treatment. But do not stop with that. The letter does not heal. The Spirit does the work. After you have made your declarations of truth, sit back and develop that "listening attitude." Listen for that "still small voice." All of a sudden, you will feel something within you. It may be a glow. It may be just a little sensing of something. It maybe a catching of the breath, or it may be light. You may see a brilliant light, or you may see a whole room light up. It may be that, like Jacob Boehme, you will be able to see behind all nature, right through the rose bushes and the grass and through the trees, through all appearances, through all forms. If you are just silent enough, you may have any kind of a mystical experience: You may find yourself tuned into God so that you really can say, "I have seen Him face to face," or you may actually have a contact with the mind that was in Christ Jesus, which is your mind.

Any of these things can happen to you—anything from the tiny touch of a feeling, up to a tremendous mystical experience. With those of us who are consciously on this path, who can live morning, noon, and night with the inspirational literature of today and yesterday, I do not know how we can miss it. Every one of us should have the most inspiring mystical experiences.

You may ask, "Of what value are they?" Not of too much value, if all your attention is focused on the experience, because that experience is an effect also. It is wonderful to have it, just as an evidence that you have touched God. It is not so wonderful, if you merely want to experience it over and over again, living for the most part, in the realm of the effect—always wanting and being satisfied with effects. That brings us to the subject of gratitude again. Let us not be thankful because we have seen a light. Let us be thankful because, in the seeing of the light, we know that we have touched God consciousness. Let us not be thankful merely because we have achieved some mystical experience and have seen through nature; but let us be grateful for this evidence of having touched God, or the Christ. Let us always express gratitude for the *cause,* not for the effect. Let us view the effect merely as an evidence.

Every demonstration you make should be treated in this way. Do not be too grateful for the demonstration, itself. Be grateful—yes, but let your gratitude be that the demonstration was a proof that, at that particular moment, you touched the Christ, that you had the awareness, the grace with which to touch It. That is the real sense of gratitude.

Coming back again to the Master's teaching, you remember that he said, "I have meat to eat that ye know not of . . . ."[7] Whosoever drinketh of the water that I shall give him shall never thirst; but the water that I shall give him shall be in him a well of water springing up into everlasting life."[8] That is the point that I have been making about gratitude. Remember, the Christ has a meat which will produce all forms of good for you. If you touch this meat which the Christ has to give you, if you once touch this wellspring of water within your own being, you will have anything and everything that is necessary to your fulfilment. But your desire then will not be so much for the forms as it will be for the continuous sense of joy that comes from knowing that this spirit within will flow forth in and as whatever form you need at any moment.

I have meat ye know not of—I have substance and awareness, a principle, so that I do not have to be dependent on thing, circumstance, or condition in the outer realm. I do not put my faith in a man, in an organization, in a job, or in an investment. If all these things were taken away, I still would have a consciousness from which all things would flow.

Let us stop living on yesterday's manna. We have been depending on the savings that we put away yesterday. We have been depending on the good will that we built up yesterday. We have been carrying over some family heritage or relying upon a reputation made in our youth. We have forgotten that all this is yesterday's manna. Yesterday's manna can be taken away from us. Therefore, let us learn right now, even while we are enjoying all the good of yesterday, that we are not living on yesterday's manna, even though we are grateful for the accumulation of good that is with us from yesterday. Our manna comes to us every day. Let us learn to be grateful for a principle which enables us, no matter what the human scene may be, to have the "meat ye know not of." Remember:

God is forever unfolding, disclosing, and revealing Itself as my individual consciousness. Therefore, all good flows out from my consciousness every moment of the day or night. God is my own consciousness. Where I am, that Consciousness is; where that Consciousness is, I am. Therefore, right at this moment, all of the good I need, and all that I shall ever need, is flowing out from the center—right where I am. All that God has, God, infinite, divine Consciousness, my consciousness, is showing forth. I do not have to fear age, because my consciousness will forever be the infinite source of my supply—God, individualized as my consciousness, will be the source and fount of my supply unto eternity.

~ 12 ~

QUESTIONS AND ANSWERS

Ed. Note: At the close of each of the class sessions on which this book is based, questions which had been submitted in writing were answered. In the mimeographed form in which *Consciousness Unfolding* has been widely read and circulated, these questions appeared at the end of several of the chapters in the book, but, in this present edition, that material has been grouped together in this one final chapter.

Question: What is the role of patience in demonstration?

Answer: If we really turn back into consciousness and feel that "click," then health and harmony will appear. But the demonstration of spiritual life may not come all at once and it may not manifest itself immediately. I am reminded of the experience of Saul of Tarsus. After years of study, the Christ came to Saul in a blinding flash. We might think that, at that moment, he would have been entirely renewed. Yet, it was another nine years before he began to go about preaching. He spent nine years living in Arabia, letting the light which had come in that blinding flash reveal and unfold itself.

We, too, might have a flash of light, perhaps on the subject of supply, and from that moment on, there might be an increase, day after day, and week after week—just enough of an increase to keep us ahead. If you consider this in terms of time, it might seem as though quite a long period elapses before the whole picture of supply reveals itself, or develops itself. It was in 1932 that I caught the vision that God is the only creative principle and that all these other ideas about wrong thinking and sin, had nothing to do with healing or supply. But it was not until 1946 that I published a book or went out to teach this truth. There were years and years of patience required while this new consciousness was forming and renewing itself.

We are likely to become impatient for results, and to feel that if we get a treatment today, we should be in heaven tomorrow. Probably, when we have attained the consciousness of the Christ all demonstrations will be instantaneous. Jesus said: "Say not ye, There yet are four months, and then cometh harvest? behold, I say unto you, Lift up your eyes, and look on the fields; for they are white already to harvest."[1] But do not forget, either, that three years passed before Jesus could finally say: "He that hath seen me hath seen the Father."[2] We know that when he was twelve years old, he had already caught the inner light, yet he did not begin his ministry until he was thirty years of age. So even Jesus had his periods of waiting, and days, months, and years, when patience was required.

I say to everyone who undertakes this work: Your consciousness must be renewed. You have been brought up in the belief that that which is out here in the world is reality, and now you are being told that your consciousness is reality. Do you think you can catch the full implication of that truth overnight? You might do so, intellectually, but sooner or later, someone is going to knock at the door and ask you to pay a bill that you cannot pay or remind you that you have a headache. And then, you will have to begin living this truth.

What we are doing is not creating miracles: We are renewing consciousness. We are dying daily. We are being reborn of the Spirit, and this rebirth comes only with patience. All these things which I have said to you are truth, but you will demonstrate them if, and as, they become an integral part of your consciousness. The healing consciousness of the practitioner is a state of consciousness that has lost its fear or hate or love of error. That is all there is to the Christ consciousness, which is your individual consciousness when you no longer fear, hate, or love error of any name or nature.

Can you drop that fear, hate, or love overnight? No, you must go through the process of being reborn, and that requires patience, stick-to-it-iveness. You may have to stand fast in the face of the very opposite appearance. It may be in the face of a very, very persistent appearance. And so you will have to stand again and again and again and say, "I am being reborn of the Spirit. I am being renewed. I am no longer going to fear, hate, or love that which is outside of me. I am going to stand on the truth that knows that consciousness is the law unto that which is outside." It takes patience.

Question: Will you discuss meditation?

Answer: When you turn within in meditation, you may not always receive the answer immediately. As a matter of fact, there may not be any answer for you to receive at that moment, but the answer will be there later, to meet any situation that arises during the day. When I meditate in the morning, nothing in particular may come to me, even though I always do feel a sense of the Presence. But an hour, or eight hours later, when someone telephones or writes, the answer is there. My constant meditation keeps me consciously one with God, at-one with the Infinite. It keeps me constantly at the point where, whatever I need, comes forth. I do not have to meditate every time a call for help comes to me because I have been meditating twenty hours out of the twenty-four. It is like keeping a line open on the switchboard. No matter who calls, the line is open.

It is all a question of at-one-ment. That is the reason I reiterate again and again: Please never undertake anything without going within and feeling that at-one-ment, which says to you, "Don't be afraid, fellow. *I* am here." Then go out, and do anything you have to do. *It* is there, and *It* is with you. The more you realize your at-one-ment with God, the more health, harmony, success, and prosperity you will experience. This at-one-ment will not make you eccentric. You will continue to enjoy life much like anyone else—movies, good books, good music, good food, and good friends. But you will acknowledge that it is your conscious oneness with God that brings out your health, harmony, and prosperity.

I never give a treatment in the commonly accepted sense of the world. My only treatment is a conscious oneness with God. If someone calls and says, "I have a problem of unemployment or health or something else," my treatment is conscious oneness with God. Nothing less than conscious oneness with God will do it.

Question: Will you discuss the Lord's Prayer?

Answer: There is some disagreement in the church world and among religious scholars as to the authenticity of the Lord's Prayer. Some scholars do not believe that Jesus ever gave the Lord's Prayer to the world, while others believe that he did. The main reason for this doubt is that the Lord's Prayer is not in keeping, apparently, with the Master's teaching. The Master did not teach that it would do us any good to ask God for any such thing as daily bread. He taught: "Your Father knoweth what things ye have need of, before ye ask him[3] . . . [and it is his] good pleasure to give you the kingdom."[4]

One Bible authority claims that when the translators came to that part of the New Testament where the disciple said: "Teach us to pray,"[5] the Master did not reply. Scholars believe that something was lost, and then when they found the page on which what is called the Lord's Prayer was written, they inserted it in that place.

Regardless of whether or not the Master did give us the Lord's Prayer, do not forget that in it there are laws just as there are in all of his teachings. In other places as well as in the Lord's Prayer, he taught the law of forgiveness, and through that law, we "forgive our debtors,"[6] for in proportion as we are able to "loose him, and let him go,"[7] does our own consciousness become free.

If parts of the Lord's Prayer–or all of it–have meaning for you, it does not matter whether or not it was a part of Jesus' actual words. Whatever is true, is true regardless of its source. We can get good wherever we find it. Personally, I find much wisdom in that particular passage: "Forgive us our debts as we forgive our debtors."[8]

Question: Should a practitioner assume responsibility for a case?

Answer: Our attitude should be the same with a human being as it would be with a dog, a cat, or a crop. The truth we know should be outwardly manifested in healing, whatever the condition may be. However, just because we accept the responsibility does not mean that we shall always be able to bring out the healing. A human being differs from plants, crops, or animals because a human being has the freedom of choice to determine his own destiny. Persistence in gross materiality may for a while cheat a person of the spiritual unfoldment of health or wealth. Those who do not lend themselves to the spiritual life, or who insist on clinging to the material sense of existence, may not always respond to spiritual healing. Why? Because if a patient is so far away from Soul as to be immersed in the senses, he may block the work of the practitioner.

When I say that the practitioner should accept the responsibility, I mean it in this way: If an individual asks for help, what is my responsibility? Is it to see a human being who needs health or reformation, or is it not rather to turn away from that picture and say, "No, God is the only reality of being," thereby refusing to do battle with the material condition, or to attempt to heal it?

The moment a person asks you for help and you look at his human condition, you are agreeing that there is a disease or a sinner. Then, after having accepted the appearance as a fact, you attempt to cure it through mind. The real treatment is: "My kingdom is not of this world."[9] Since my kingdom, my spiritual kingdom, is not of the mortal, material world, I am not here to reform or heal a mortal. I must look away from mortality and behold the spiritual man. In that sense, then, it is my responsibility as a practitioner not to accept the evidence of the senses, even when that evidence testifies to a sick or dying mortal. That is my sole responsibility.

The responsibility of the *patient* is receptivity. In so far as possible he must be willing to give up his material sense of existence to accept the spiritual. He must not merely be willing to have a heart that was diagnosed as imperfect made perfect, but also be willing to turn to the spiritual sense of living, at least to *desire* the spiritual life. If he is unwilling to give up his mortal sense of existence, if he wants to cling to that and to look upon the practitioner as an aspirin with which to ease the pain, the practitioner may fail, and the patient may fail. The Master taught that if they did not believe you or accept you, you should leave them.

Question: How do you attain an inner conviction of faith?

Answer: The real sense of faith is an impartation from God within you. Ask for faith, as you would turn within and ask for a revelation of harmony, health, or supply. Faith is not a human quality. Faith is divine. When people have a faith that has come to them from the outer world, it is not really faith; it is a blind belief. Faith is of God. Faith is understanding. You have faith that 2x2 are 4, and it does not change. That faith is based on your understanding of the laws of mathematics.

I have faith that the law of God is the only law unto my being. I understand why that law works. I have seen it operate. So I have faith in it, as in 2x2 equaling 4. Let your faith be a God-faith, not *your* faith. "I can of mine own self do nothing."[10] Turn within and let faith come. And when it comes from within, you are grounded on the rock, and nothing will ever lead you astray.

The spiritual sense of life comes from within. Your spiritual sense touches the kingdom of God, and finds that, in the outer realm, all that is necessary to the demonstration is added. As you make your transition from dependence on the outer to dependence on the inner, you are really turning to the original creative Principle of existence, which is your own consciousness.

The world believes that the mother and the father are the creators of a child. But no parents ever created a body. The state of consciousness of that child brought forth his own body. In the same way, your particular state of consciousness and my particular state of consciousness have brought forth the bodies we have at present. If a child were brought up from the beginning with the knowledge that we are gaining in this study, then he would not be affected by any of the human beliefs, whether of health, wealth, war, or any problem in the world today.

You learn to know your own being only in the degree that you know what God is. God is life—your life. God is consciousness—your consciousness. You are fed from within. You are maintained and sustained from within. All the beliefs of the world have no power, or jurisdiction over you. In proportion as you consciously accept this truth and allow yourself to receive treatment, these impartations of truth take form within your own being.

Everything I am saying here is a treatment; it is the truth of being flowing out. There must be a continuous flowing of truth out from the center of your being to your outer awareness. That is treatment. Therefore, you must always be in a state of receptivity. In all my writings, watch how many times I say, "Be a state of receptivity. Develop a state of receptivity. Develop the listening ear." Why? So as to become receptive to the truth, so that you may be able to hear the voice of God.

What has the voice of God to say to you? *"I Am your life; I Am always with you; all that I have is thine."* That is treatment. That is prayer. That is communion. That is the "meat" that the world knows nothing of. That is the substance of your bones, of your flesh, of your muscles, and of your strength and intelligence: *"I have meat to eat that ye know not of."* [11]

Rebirth begins the moment you begin to be fed from within. There is no kind of material food, no kind of vitamin, that will keep your personal self here for very long. But there is a bread, a wine, and a water; there is a divine substance, which is your own consciousness of being. This will rebuild and bring you to a state of unfoldment so that five years from now you will look back at yourself and not know yourself.

The harmony of your being emanates from your own consciousness. There is no use going back and blaming your father or your mother. There is nothing wrong with your body that has ever been inherited. If there is anything wrong with the outer vehicle, then make the correction within, through your realization that you do not have a personal consciousness to be influenced by the beliefs of the world. God is your consciousness, and God is the substance of your being, of your body, and of your home. Will not that kind of treatment bring forth the realization that I and the Father are one, and that the place whereon I stand is holy ground?

Everything that comes to you must come from within your own being, or else the Master was entirely wrong when he said: "The kingdom of God is within you." [12] What reason is there for believing that there is a presence and a power outside of your own consciousness? "Before Abraham was, I am. . . ."[13] Lo, I am with you always even unto the end of the world."[14] Then, when did error begin in your experience? It never did begin! You have merely accepted universal beliefs, and that is the only error there is. I have called it "hypnotism," a universal belief in a power or presence apart from God.

Therefore, all the good, unto the end of the world, is flowing in and through and *as* you and me at this very moment. No power from without can enter "to defile or make a lie." Nothing can enter my consciousness and take over. Why? It is God. God is my consciousness, and how could anything enter Infinity? Is there anything outside of Infinity? Let this truth reveal itself from the Father within, and you will find harmony and peace. You will find evolution, and you will find reincarnation. You will find a new body being incarnated for you, a new state of consciousness being developed for you. You will really be able to say, "I am not the same this year as I was last year. I have died to mortal beliefs. I have been reborn of the Spirit."

But no one can do this for you, and no one can come into this for you. It is a conscious process which takes place in your consciousness, and whatever takes place in your consciousness will externalize itself in your experience.

Question: When you go into the silence, do you always feel you should make affirmations about God?

Answer: No; it depends upon where you are in consciousness. When you attempt to enter the silence, if you do not immediately touch God consciousness, then it is wise to realize God as life, God as love, and so on; and then settle down into the attitude of listening. This applies to my own meditations. Sometimes when I go into meditation, I am immediately in this consciousness, and nothing is necessary in the way of statements of truth. Sometimes, when I am called upon for healing work, I cannot get the sense of oneness for some reason or other, and I must sit for as much as an hour, or two, or three, before achieving that sense of conscious oneness. Do not let anyone, ever, put you into a routine. If you do not feel your oneness, be willing to work until you reach it. If you do feel your oneness, you can stop in that second.

Question: Do we have individual spiritual bodies?

Answer: We have a spiritual body. Paul says we are all "members of that one body,"[15] but the body is spiritual, and it is infinite in form. Do not try to measure Infinity by your idea of It. You are trying to think of the infinite, spiritual body in terms of time and space. There is only one body, just as there is only one sun in the skies. When you see sunbeams, that is only the appearance. There is only one sunbeam, just as there is only one sun. There is only one body: It is a spiritual body and it is infinitely manifest.

Question: How do you make your patient comfortable, when called upon for treatment?

Answer: You don't! You get at-one with God, and let God make the patient comfortable. No matter who your patient is, if you achieve your conscious oneness with

God and feel it, your patient is well. He will let you know that he is healed.

Question: Did Jesus break the law of karma?

Answer: Yes, and you can break the law of karma. But that does not mean that it does not exist. When Jesus indicated that as ye sow, so shall ye reap, he was referring to the law of karma. Karma says that whatever your thought or your conduct is today, you will reap tomorrow, next year, or in your next lifetime. But you can break this law. You can break it by turning away, and living anew through repentance. If a person is sinning and then has a spiritual vision, his previous life disappears; it has passed out of his consciousness; he has broken the law of cause and effect. With that past life wiped out, there can no longer be any effect from it. The word "karma" is but an oriental word for a universal law, the law of cause and effect.

Jesus broke the law of karma. Whenever he healed a sick man, he broke the law of karma. Every time a metaphysician heals a case, he is breaking the law of karma. Not for the world, did Jesus break it, but for himself—although his demonstration is our assurance. You live differently from your fellow man if you know spiritual law. If you live in accordance with divine law, you cannot sin. A sin is the violation of a principle. When you are living according to principle, and when you are living in a state of spiritual consciousness, you do not need the Ten Commandments. You are not in need of the laws which have been passed against stealing when you are living according to principle. You do not need laws against breaking traffic rules: When you have love in your heart, you cannot drive beyond a limit that is safe for others driving on the same highway.

We must read Scripture in the light of what, why, and when. Moses took the Hebrews who had lived with no education or culture, and as slaves under Pharaoh, out of Egypt. He led them out into the wilderness, and found that all of a sudden they were living like wild beasts and that they required specific regulations, and penalties for the violation of these regulations. In this light, therefore, scriptural events take on new meaning. We can see the reason for the Ten Commandments being given to the Hebrews as they then were.

When we come to the Sermon on the Mount, we are told that the pure in heart shall see God. It does not say anything about being good, but only being pure in heart, pure in consciousness, pure in conviction. If you are really pure through conviction and not for the purpose of reward, but because you have no other sense, no other consciousness than that of purity, you are then really approaching spiritual consciousness.

Question: What qualifications should a person who is not interested in spiritual matters have in order to get the benefit of treatment?

Answer: He is still entitled to treatment. It may be the very thing which is pushing him into spirituality. How will a man ever get to know something about that of which he knows nothing? Usually, he is driven by sin, disease, or lack. That is what is driving him. And that, then, is what brings him into the spiritual world where he finds healing.

Now the only reason he ever thought of a spiritual teaching was for that healing—not because of spiritual consciousness. It may be, however, that through a healing, some degree of spirituality is opened in his consciousness, and from then on he begins the ascent on the spiritual path. On the other hand, it may be that he will be left entirely untouched by the healing and when he is sick again, he will come back just for another healing. It may take his being healed from three to five times before he is touched at all. Then, suddenly, as one of those healings occurs, he begins his ascent.

We are not to look upon the human scene and try to heal and reform it. We do not take into consideration the fact that a person is a Catholic, Jew, or Protestant. Jesus healed all. And that is why we go into prisons. We know that we are going among people who have committed serious offenses, but we must go just the same. Most of those people have not a thought of spirituality. They have in mind only trying to get rid of some pain or discord, or trying to make a contact which will help them get out of their prison. Their motives are entirely selfish. But it was through my experience working spiritually with prisoners that I discovered the foundation of all the work that I am now doing: The basic truth of any spiritual teaching is that God is the mind of the individual—God is his life, his Soul.

It is not our function to judge whether those who call upon us for help want loaves and fishes—healing for healing's sake. Our function is to wipe out the human picture and say, "There is nothing there but God." At that level of consciousness, even if the patient says, "I am worse," and goes on to say, "I am dying!" our function is not to try to help a human being, but to look through that picture and say, "There is nothing there but God, the divine reality of being."

Even when people come to a spiritual teaching only for a healing, I believe it is God bringing them into it. Some day truth will break through. Healing is only a matter of consciousness. One of the problems we have is that people want to use spiritual truth for healing, and then the minute they have their healing, they continue right along in the old way of living, instead of saying, "I have seen this healing. Now, will you show me how it is done? What must I do?" We, in this work, are not trying to build up reputations for ourselves as successful practitioners with a big practice. Rather, we are trying to show forth the principle that is available to anyone if he will develop his consciousness. The ideal attitude for any student or practitioner in this healing work is to give the patient some kind of truth that he can take with him, so that he will understand something about it, and then continue to give him truth as he is able to take it.

Question: Is it necessary for a person to desire healing? If not, can we help him?

Answer: You can, sometimes. Whether you can always do so, I would not be able to say. I have not seen it done in too many cases on a complete scale, but it can be done sometimes. If I knew that a member of my family or a friend, even though not interested in this work, were going through trying times, I would take up work with the idea of bringing him out of his particular claim and probably of opening his consciousness to truth. But whether it would always succeed, I do not know. Often, he cannot get the benefit when his mind is closed to it. My own position is that I would give him the benefit of all the truth I know, even if it seemed to have no effect.

However, in such a case, I would not hold a practitioner responsible for results. One can only do the best one can, and if there is some receptivity, the healing will come through.

Question: Can we give help to those who have passed on?

Answer: Has anything happened to them? Is it not that we are giving the help to ourselves about them? They do not claim to have anything wrong with them. They may not even know that we think they have passed on. They may have no idea that they have passed on. And they have not. Heaven forbid that anyone should ever pass on! It would be proof that there is no God. God is life eternal, and that life is yours. Nothing can ever happen to that life. No, one thing that you are always aware of is that you cannot die. Never will you believe that you have died. You may think you are going to die, but you will never come to the place of dying.

What about those who are not with us any longer? Only to our sense is that so. We are the ones who are blind, and so we do not see them. We do not have to help them. They are all right now. We lift ourselves to the point of realizing that they are already in God consciousness. They know it. It is we who are entertaining a belief that they are dead and so it is we, who need the treatment. If we could have given ourselves enough treatment before we accepted their passing, we might have prevented it.

When a practitioner prevents a passing on, that is what happens. He has raised himself to the place where he knows that death is not a possibility. He knows that there never was a danger to a patient. He knows that the only thing to handle is a belief that someone can die. He knows that life is eternal. We cannot arrive at any degree of spiritual being, body, or universe, by an appraisal of the human scene. Always remember that. Never look at the human scene, and from it, try to judge of spiritual reality. You may look at a cemetery and say, "There is death"; you may look at hospitals, and be sure there is disease; but if you want to know the truth, get quiet within your own being and let God reveal spiritual truth to you. Then you will find that in the history of reality, there never was sin, disease, death, lack, or limitation.

Those who believe in spiritualism are convinced that death takes place. They say that life is eternal, but they are speaking of a life after death. In spiritualism, there is no life eternal on earth; there is no body that is immortal. The spiritualist must first accept the death of the body, that is, a transitional state called "death," in order to manifest eternal life.

Our sense of eternal life has nothing to do with life after death. Our sense of pre-existence has nothing to do with life before birth. Our sense of pre-existence of immortality, of life eternal, has nothing to do with time or space. It has to do with *now. Now* are we the Sons of God; *now* am I life eternal. In that nowness, there is no past, there is no present, there is no future. There is just the continuous unfolding of consciousness—just as we go from nursery school to elementary school, and then to high school and college. It is just an unfolding consciousness, and in it there is no past and there is no future, when we look on it in its wholeness.

Is it possible then to receive communications from those who, to sense, have passed on? Certainly, since they have *not* passed on. They are right here where they have always been. They are always a part of our consciousness. If ever you come into agreement with the teaching of Jesus Christ, which is immortality and life eternal, you will never, never believe that anyone has died or has left consciousness or has left your consciousness. It will be like the woman who says, "My husband is in China." She is not grieving over that. She continues to enjoy his integrity, goodness, and culture. Just because he is out of her physical sight, does that mean death or separation? It means only that he is out of physical sight. Even though she does not see him daily, she is occasioned no grief because of her conviction that he is still with her.

So, as you go higher and higher, you realize more and more that there is no death. Then it makes no difference if, for some reason, your loved one has gone out of your sight. You will feel no sense of separation. You will still have the sense of his presence.

The whole secret lies in your ability to understand that we exist as states of consciousness. If I am in your consciousness now, I can continue to be a part of your consciousness, whether I am in Los Angeles or in New York, or sitting in your living room. And you can be a part of mine. With that understanding, there is no reason why we could not communicate with each other, even at a distance, if there were any occasion for it. I am sure that many of you have had just that experience.

That which we call "mother," "father," or "child," is really God. It is eternal life made manifest. How can God die? How can "the mind that was in Christ Jesus" go anywhere? It is always omnipresent being. Death, itself, is based on the belief that human beings were born at some point in time. We are refuting this through spiritual wisdom. What is the whole secret of spiritual healing? It is that we are infinite, individual, spiritual being.

Then is there death? Is there a passing on? No, no, no! Any sense we may have of a death or a passing on is our acceptance of a universally imposed belief—that is all. Begin to understand that God is your wife, your husband, and your children; in other words, life eternal made manifest is the only person you know. You must do that in treatment, so why not in thinking about those closely related to you?

Death is based on the belief that you and I are human beings and that we were born at some point in time. Eternal life is based on the spiritual revelation that you and I are life eternal. "Before Abraham was, I am. Unto the end of the world, lo, I am with you." How can you reconcile death, or passing, or separation with such assurance? Since that is true, why is it not possible for Jesus to appear to those who are in tune or at-one with his state of consciousness? Why should he not appear, even in physical form, in the sense of being a divine presence and protection? Why should not Moses appear to those of the Judaic faith, if that is their concept of deific power? Why was Jesus enabled to make the demonstration on the Mount of Transfiguration? How was it possible to bring back Moses and Elijah and Elias? They had not gone any place! They never were human beings who had died. They were always the divine Consciousness Itself, individually manifest and expressed.

If you want to demonstrate health and harmony for yourself or for your loved ones, immortal life for yourself and for them, give up the belief that your wife or your husband or your children are human beings. Begin to accept that which you must use in your treatment, and that is that you are the Christ of God. You are immortal and eternal. Begin to believe that about yourself and your family. Have you ever given a treatment without the declaration that your patient is immortal, eternal, and the manifestation of God? Is that not included in every treatment? How can the eternal manifestation of God die?

The only death, then, is our acceptance of the universal belief that we are human beings. From there, we go on and accept the rest of the belief that we have three score years and ten to live under scriptural law, or sixty-four to sixty-seven years to live as an insurance statistic. We bring ourselves under those universal beliefs by our acceptance of them as law.

But as you gain the conviction that the words you use in treatment are true, if you really can gain the conviction that I am life eternal, that all that God is, I am, how can there be a death? Death will be the last thing that is overcome, and the only way that it will be overcome is when you analyze your treatment and say, "Do I really *believe* it, or am I just *saying* it?" When you accept the truth of the eternality and infinity of your being, you cannot come under the belief of death.

Let us think, now, in terms of God as truth and see what new idea regarding your individual being will be revealed to you. If we think of God as truth, and if we think of ourselves as the manifestation or the revelation or unfoldment of that Truth, can we at the same time think of ourselves in terms of living or of dying? Can Truth die? Then, have we not been thinking of God as some kind of a limited being, and of ourselves as some kind of a human being?

Let us take this idea and ponder on what it would really mean to know that God is truth, and what Jesus meant when he said: "I am . . . truth." Because if you can understand the truth of being, you never again will be disturbed by the idea of mortality. You will know no such thing in your life as death.

There is nothing limited about God, Truth; therefore, there is nothing of a personal or limited nature about the infinite and individual Truth: *I* am the way; *I* am the truth; *I* am life eternal. As truth, you cannot be confined to time, place, or space; and *you are truth*. You are following the teaching of the Master, Jesus Christ: "Before Abraham was, I am. . . . Lo, I, *Truth*, will be with you until the end of the world." As Truth, you cannot be limited in form or in expression. As infinite Truth, there is nothing outside your own being to act upon you for good or evil in any way. All power, law, cause, and effect are the manifestation and activity of your own being appearing as your universe. That is what you are when you are declaring: *I* am truth; *I* am life eternal; *I* am Soul; *I* am Spirit; all that God is, *I* am.

Close your eyes and say "I." Then remember that at six years of age you could have closed your eyes and said "I," in exactly the same way in which you are saying it now, and it would have been the same "I" that you are talking about at this moment. That "I" has never changed, and it will never change and never die, but it will unfold infinitely. If you ever permit your body to slip out, you will find that *I am* standing right back there watching it. To catch even a glimpse of yourself as Truth, will destroy all sense of discord, inharmony, ill health, and the grave.

This is likewise so in understanding the statement: "I am the light of the world."[16] Can you ever think of a light becoming dark, or dying, or passing out? Or going somewhere? Take the word right into meditation and see yourself as light. No longer, then, will you accept a sense of limitation.

By understanding ourselves as truth and as light, we shall gain an entirely new idea of Self. Then, instead of being concerned with the appearance, we shall turn away from it and gain the spiritual idea that is the light of the world. We cannot reform, heal, or change whatever the human mind thinks of itself. Do not attempt to improve the old concept of self. Rather, gain the new idea that Jesus gave us two thousand years ago: "I am the way; I am the truth; I am the life."[17] How can you destroy any of that?

Question: Why should a person be "on the mountain top," and then down in the depths?

Answer: These experiences of ups and downs are natural. Never in the history of the world has anyone been on the mountain top and stayed there. Even Jesus had to go away for forty days at a time. But through the study and practice of meditation and inspirational living, you approach a level which is not a mountain top but is a high place of understanding.

The degrees of ups and downs are the outcome of our human experiences, and the consciousness which we should attain is one which does not react to human experiences by going up too high, nor by descending too low. The Christ consciousness which Jesus had was not of this world; yet while not being of this world, it operated as his human experience. His state of consciousness became operative as individual consciousness and could be applied to the things of this world, although he, himself, said that his kingdom was not of this world.

The Hindu mystic may let his body die and may call that a spiritual demonstration insofar as "his kingdom is not of this world." But Jesus said, in effect: "My kingdom is not of this world, and therefore, I lift my body up to that consciousness where my kingdom is, and I show forth my body as a spiritual body." This great truth is illumination.

This is a world of reality. *Here* is the world of reality. Right here and now is God's kingdom. This is not an illusion: This is God's kingdom. The way we look at it, what we see through our eyes—that is the illusion. But the world, itself, is reality. That is why we do not heal or improve it. We merely change our concept of it, because it, itself, is perfect right here and now. You are the very Christ of God, the very life of God, made manifest. We see you through the eyes of human concept, imperfect, but *you are perfect.*

A Hindu mystic looks at this "illusion," and closes his eyes and says, "This is not reality." That is not correct. This that you see is not illusion: The illusion is the way you see it. When you see railroad tracks, that is not an illusion. The illusion lies in seeing them coming together. But the tracks, themselves, are very real. You are not illusion. You are the presence of God, but what we are seeing with our eyes is illusion. We are seeing an illusory concept of you. So what do we have to change— you, or our *concept* of you? The Hindu mystic says, "This world is illusion, so I will not bother to heal the body at all. . . ." But the body is not illusion. It is the temple of God, according to the teaching of Christ Jesus.

Let us never forget this: *This is a spiritual universe.* This is the kingdom of God, and the illusion is not this world, but the universal *concept* of this world. The only place this concept must and can be changed is in the practitioner's thought. When the concept is healed in the practitioner's thought, the patient responds. Why? Because the practitioner's thought is the only place where he can behold an illusion.

When we go within with a desire to understand the spiritual kingdom, we can expect to see increased understanding take form as improved conditions. We go within and ask for the spiritual kingdom, and then it appears outwardly right here and now. When it does not appear, it is because your inner vision has not yet been changed: The light of the Christ has not yet touched it. See the world as Spirit. Seeing it as matter is the illusion. The world is not matter. *This is a spiritual universe.* Sin and disease are not actualities; they are illusion or mortal concept. Once you see that, you will never again try to heal the outside, as if it actually were something you could heal.

Question: Will you discuss gratitude?

Answer: Gratitude has been emphasized a great deal in the sense of being grateful for healings and for help. When gratitude is correctly understood, it is an important part of this or of any spiritual teaching. In our human ignorance, we see sin, death, disease, lack, and limitation. Through our illumined state of consciousness, we see reality as it is. It would be a sorry person, indeed, who did not have a sense of gratitude for whatever or whoever it is that lifts him up to see reality.

I have said before, in speaking of tithing, that where tithing or gratitude is expressed in the hope of a reward, it is a farce. When gratitude or tithing has to do with the expectancy of some good in the future, then it is useless. But when gratitude is expressed or tithing is practiced because of having received an illumination, or for a certain measure of understanding that has come, or for improvement that has come through understanding, then it is true gratitude. When a person tithes his income at ten, five, or even one percent, out of a pure sense of gratitude for what he has received of light and the manifestation of that light in his outer experience, that sense of gratitude is spiritual in quality. But when gratitude is tinged with a sense of self-seeking, in the sense of, "If I am grateful enough and pay out enough, good will come to me," then such gratitude is folly, and might better not be expressed.

Gratitude, especially as expressed in tithing, has another meaning. When a person can take a percentage of his earnings and say, "This is not coming from me; this is part of what God is expending for Its own activity. I am merely the transfer agent for it," that sense of tithing and gratitude soon shows itself forth as improved earnings, opportunities, and income.

The day is coming when we will not only give our church or spiritual activity some part of our income, feeling that we are the transfer agents for God's support of Its own activity, but we shall take that same attitude with respect to every demand that is made upon us. If a demand is made upon us for the support of our family, for a gift to someone on his birthday, for some charitable enterprise, or even for our income tax, and if we can catch the idea that this demand is not being made upon us as a person or upon our income, but that it is made on the Christ for which we are acting as the transfer agent, we shall find abundance flowing to us and out from us—even to the extent of having most of our salary left at the end of the week. The supply appears from many avenues to fulfil those needs.

Never should we accept any demand as being made upon you or upon me as a person, any more than we would accept a demand upon us personally for healing. When you ask a practitioner for a healing, you know that he is not giving you anything of himself. He merely rests in his understanding or state of spiritual consciousness, which then appears as healing of the body or of the mind. In the same way, money is no less spiritual than truth. If once we can see that God is the underlying substance of everything that is appearing to our consciousness, that all that exists is our consciousness unfolding, disclosing, and revealing Itself in individual form, why should not money be just as infinite and just as plentiful as the leaves on the trees?

The point we are emphasizing is that God is the consciousness of the individual, and that consciousness is unfolding the infinity of its own being as person, place, or thing. It is all your consciousness unfolding. If we grasp that, and if we do not set anything apart and say, "This is material," or, "That is material," and if once we come to realize that God, our individual consciousness, is infinite and is just as infinite in expressing and manifesting money as it is in growing our gardens, in that degree will we overcome any sense of limitation in our finances. Let us clear up these things. Let us eliminate the belief that one part of our world is spiritual and that another is material.

The same thing applies to the body. Let us get back to Jesus' teaching that God is the mind, Soul, and life of all being, and that the body is a *form* of life. If the body is that, then loaves and fishes are also forms of that one life, and so is gold in the fishes' mouths. Gradually, then, we come to the realization of Spirit as the only substance. It is something of a shock to the human mind to be told that money and potatoes and rocks are spiritual. Nevertheless, as we imbibe this truth, we shall become accustomed to the idea that, if God is consciousness and God is infinite, then consciousness is infinite. Everything that exists must exist as the form or formation of consciousness, so that it must be just as spiritual as consciousness itself; it must be just as infinite, just as eternal, just as omnipresent.

As we gain that insight, we bring forth the body as Jesus did, and say, "I am not a ghost; this is I, appearing with my same body. Thrust your hand in and feel the spear wound. It is the same body." When you agree that the body of Jesus, the body of the Christ, is spiritual, you will have to agree that any body, regardless of its form, is Spirit, Consciousness, and therefore infinite. With this acceptance and realization, you find that the body is being constantly renewed. Instead of being a piece of matter wearing out, it is consciousness, continuously unfolding and disclosing itself. The body is renewed minute by minute, as we gain the consciousness that God is the consciousness of the individual, and that Consciousness is forever unfolding, disclosing, and revealing itself in and as individual forms. This realization reveals the immortality of the body.

"I and my Father are one."[18] Spirit and body are *one.* As we understand oneness, and see that our body is our consciousness *formed*, then we overcome the world's mesmeric belief about body. We, as consciousness, maintain our body in health, harmony, and youth. There will be no aging in the realization that mind and body are one. We are dealing with God, which is one. We are dealing with God as consciousness. The body must be as infinite as consciousness. Is it material, this consciousness? No, then it cannot be divided. You cannot take Spirit and measure it in a material form. You must lift consciousness higher into the spiritual idea by going into meditation.

We must outgrow the belief of finiteness and of numbers. There are no numbers in God. There is only one number. We must see what it means to have infinite forms and varieties of one. We must see oneness, infinitely formed. We must not see body as something separate. We must catch a spiritual sense of body through meditation.

Question: What are the techniques for meditation?

Answer: The only technique that works for me is to pay no attention to any thoughts that come and go. Let them come and let them go, not honoring them with your attention. They are world thoughts. Sit, with your mind centered on the question, "What is God?" and keep it there. If thoughts disturb or intrude, bring your mind gently back to your question. Your meditation periods will unfold, develop, and grow with practice. Take a question into your meditation: What is God? What is the Christ? What is spiritual man? What is the spiritual sense of supply? What is the spiritual sense of harmony or of peace?

Question: When you are meditating, do you use positive statements, affirmations, or do you remain silent, keeping thought on some question or on a single idea?

Answer: When you meditate, take a question and ponder it. As you ponder it, suddenly, you feel yourself in God consciousness. From that moment on, listen. The real meditation is just listening. All any of the rest of it is, is for the purpose of arriving at that point of listening. When you are listening, you are meditating.

The object of meditation is opening consciousness to God. It has no other object. We do not meditate for the purpose of seeing or hearing "something." It is true that often a statement does come to us, or that a light is seen. Sometimes, too, a person is completely surrounded by light or he finds his room is filled with light. It may be that he receives a direct impartation either in scriptural or metaphysical language, or in some form absolutely original to himself. But none of this is necessary.

Let me explain this again, because meditation is so important in this work. The whole object of meditation is opening consciousness. You do not have to experience any occult phenomena. The only reason we have a process of meditation is because in our occidental world, very few people have been taught to turn to God, to be still and to listen to God. We are trying, through meditation, to reverse that situation. We are trying to learn to say, as did Jesus: "I can of mine own self do nothing . . ."[19] the Father that dwelleth in me, he doeth the works."[20] The technique of meditation is the process by which we open our consciousness and let the Father come in and take over. There is no virtue in saying,

"The Father doeth the works," if you do not have a Father to do them. Improved conditions in the outer world are the direct response to opening your consciousness and asking the Father to flow in.

The Father does not have to flow in with words. I do not always have a response in words; sometimes it is only a feeling. I know, then, that the Father is there. Anything that conveys the feeling of the presence of God is all that is necessary. Sometimes, that silence lasts only a minute, or half a minute. After you have meditated for some length of time and have learned to turn within for divine guidance, you may find that meditation has become habitual, and that you do not have to sit down to meditate before driving your automobile, walking to the office, cleaning the house, or attending to any business at hand. All you have to do is to look up and smile, and find that that opens your consciousness. At first, it may not work that rapidly and we use this process of meditation to "clear the way." Once you do arrive at this second stage, it is not then necessary to stop and sit down so often for meditation. It is enough to keep that listening ear open.

I have often stressed: Do not do too much reading. When you come to a passage in whatever it is you are reading that stands out, sit and meditate on it; ponder it; get the inner meaning of it.

We need inner enlightenment concerning the outer world. When we open our consciousness, we see it as it is. We do not change it. The outer world is already spiritual and perfect. It is already the manifestation of Consciousness, but we are seeing it through a glass darkly. As illumination comes to us and we see with inner vision, we cease to be among those who having eyes see not, and those who having ears hear not. Our inner eyes begin to discern reality.

Nothing changes in the world. The same old world goes on, but now in a more harmonious way. We do not see what the world calls "angels" running around, but the people we meet are angels to us, and we become so to them.

Jesus said: "The kingdom of God is within you."[21] That is not literally true, but the real truth is that *you are the kingdom of God.* See the "kingdom of God" as consciousness and as consciousness formed. It is neither external nor internal: It is both. In one sense, it certainly is appearing externally, as for example, in the people who are appearing to us. But spiritually, they are not external to us: They are a part of our own consciousness, or how else would we be aware of them? We are living in what appears to be two worlds, the human and the spiritual. We are told to be in this world, but not of it. Jesus said, "I pray not that thou shouldest take them out of the world,"[22] but that the evil be taken out of your concept, that the error be taken from your concept.

Consciousness cannot be confined within anything and be infinite. So, actually, consciousness, being infinite, is the *in* and the *out* to all there is. Then that consciousness is ever being manifested as creation. It is *in* it; it is *of* it; it is *from* it; it is *as* it. But actually, it is consciousness appearing. It is as though we could take this roomful of air, and make forms out of the air. These would still be air, and would not be in or out of the air. Literally, they would be forms of air. So it is with consciousness.

Consciousness is infinite substance. Because consciousness is infinite, its formations, which we call creation, must be infinitely appearing because the very substance of which they are formed is infinite. Is this not true of the mind of a composer? Is not his consciousness of music appearing in infinite combinations of notes? Does not the consciousness of a mathematician appear in an infinity of numbers and combination of numbers and formulae; or the artist, painting hundreds and thousands of strokes, an infinity of artistic knowledge appearing as paintings? The same is true of these words you are reading. Are they not the very consciousness of truth, itself, appearing in an infinity of words, sentences, statements, examples, parables, and illustrations? That same consciousness of truth can go on and write hundreds, thousands of books, if egotism does not enter in to make the writer think that he is doing it of himself. As long as I can keep my consciousness open to the oneness of mind and let it flow, there is no limit to the books that can be written on the subject of truth. Truth, being infinite, must be infinitely expressed.

It is better to let truth unfold as your consciousness, rather than to approach this study from a purely intellectual point of view, questioning every statement in the light of human reason. The greatest teaching is from inner unfoldment. Be willing to be "taught of God." That is why I am stressing so much the idea of meditation, of inner unfoldment, of God appearing as your own individual consciousness. That is the reason I also ask you not to read through pages and pages of books from cover to cover without stopping. Read until some kind of an idea develops or unfolds. Then ponder that and let the light of truth come from within.

The real function of a teacher is to free the student from the teacher. That can be done only as you learn to let this truth unfold. Whatever is told you *intellectually* will not be effective spiritual teaching. No one can tell you what God is. I can say to you that God is infinite consciousness revealing Itself, but it would be sheer folly for you to think that I have told you what God is. You will know what God is, only as that knowledge unfolds to you from within.

In the occidental world, we have not been taught to go within. The experience is new to most people. Some have been taught to learn certain statements, affirmations, and denials, and to repeat them. They have not been taught to go to the kingdom of their own consciousness. Most people are not trained to meditate. But I know this: There is no real teaching from without. The only teacher who is going to prove of any lasting value in your life is the one who can lead you back to the kingdom of your own mind and the realm of your own Soul and there let the divine Infinite come forth.

My function is not so much to teach the letter of truth. However, there are three points of the letter which it is important that you remember: the nature of God; the nature of individual being; and the nature of error, which we are forever battling in this human world of sin, disease, and death, lack and limitation. Then we shall learn not so much to battle these, as to meet them by seeing *through* them. When you understand the nature of treatment and of prayer, you experience the nature of the Christ. The Christ is nothing in the way of words; it is a *feeling*. It is an assurance of the Presence. It comes forth from our own consciousness through meditation and unfoldment. Then you experience God unfolding as your own individual consciousness, and that is the purpose of the Infinite Way.

SCRIPTURAL REFERENCES

Chapter 1
1. Luke 15:31
2. Mark 7:16
3. Luke 18:17
4. Matthew 5:25
5. 1 John 4:4
6. Luke 15:31
7. John 10:30
8. Exodus 3:5
9. Psalms 139:8
10. John 8:11
11. Galatians 5:7
12. John 5:8
13. 1 Corinthians 15:50
14. 1 Corinthians 13:12
15. John 6:1–10
16. John 6:10, 11
17. John 6:12–20
18. John 6:24–26
19. Luke 12:22
20. John 6:27
21. John 6:28, 29
22. John 6:30–33
23. John 6:34, 35
24. John 6:36–38
25. John 10:34
26. John 6:40
27. John 6:40
28. John 6:41
29. John 6:42–45
30. John 6:45

Chapter 2
1. John 14:27
2. Isaiah 55:8
3. Mark 4:39
4. Zechariah 4:6
5. Philippians 4:7
6. Luke 17:21
7. John 14:27
8. Luke 12:22, 29, 30, 27
9. 1 Corinthians 13:1
10. John 6:46
11. John 6:51
12. John 6:53
13. John 6:60, 61
14. John 6:63, 64
15. John 6:64, 65
16. John 6:66
17. John 7:7
18. Philippians 4:7
19. Matthew 4:1–4
20. Luke 12:22
21. Luke 12:31
22. Matthew 4:5–7
23. Matthew 4:8–11

Chapter 3
1. John 14:27
2. Luke 10:27
3. Mark 4:39
4. John 14:6
5. John 10:10

Chapter 3 (Continued)
    6. John 14:6
    7. John 14:9
    8. John 5:30
    9. John 7:16
  10. John 5:31
  11. John 14:12
  12. Luke 12:30
  13. Luke 12:32

Chapter 4
    1. John 10:30
    2. Galatians 2:20
    3. Psalms 121:1
    4. Genesis 1:31
    5. John 4:32
    6. Matthew 15:11
    7. John 8:32
    8. John 4:32
    9. John 4:14
  10. John 6:63
  11. John 4:32
  12. John 4:14

Chapter 5
    1. 1 Corinthians 2:14
    2. 1 Corinthians 13:1
    3. John 10:18
    4. Matthew 28:20
    5. John 4:35
    6. John 5:30
    7. John 14:10
    8. Luke 17:2

Chapter 6
    1. Matthew 7:20
    2. John 14:12
    3. John 7:24
    4. Galatians 6:7
    5. Job 4:8

Chapter 6 (Continued)
    6. Galatians 6:7
    7. Joel 2:12
    8. Ezekiel 33:11
    9. Matthew 5:25
  10. John 19:11
  11. 1 Corinthians 3:16
  12. Luke 15:31

Chapter 7
    1. 2 Corinthians 3:6

Chapter 8
    1. John 18:36
    2. John 4:32
    3. Mark 8:18
    4. John 14:6
    5. John 4:32
    6. John 4:14
    7. Mark 3:33, 35

Chapter 9
    1. Isaiah 2:22
    2. Luke 12:25
    3. Matthew 5:36
    4. Luke 24:39
    5. Matthew 26:52
    6. Luke 23:34
    7. Acts 17:24
    8. Revelation 22:5
    9. Isaiah 2:22
  10. John 12:45
  11. John 10:27
  12. Acts 17:24
  13. 2 Corinthians 5:1
  14. Romans 8:17
  15. Matthew 28:20

Chapter 10
    1. Isaiah 26:3

Chapter 10 (Continued)
2. Proverbs 3:5, 6
3. Psalms 138:8
4. John 1:11
5. John 8:58
6. Matthew 28:20
7. 1 Kings 19:12
8. Luke 22:42
9. Galatians 2:20
10. Mark 12:31
11. Mark 12:30
12. Luke 15:31
13. Isaiah 2:22
14. 1 John 3:2
15. Philippians 4:7

Chapter 11
1. Matthew 11:4, 5
2. John 8:32
3. John 14:9
4. John 10:30
5. John 8:58
6. Matthew 28:20
7. John 4:32
8. John 4:14

Chapter 12
1. John 4:35
2. John 14:9
3. Matthew 6:8
4. Luke 12:32
5. Luke 11:1
6. Matthew 6:12
7. John 11:44
8. Matthew 6:12
9. John 18:36
10. John 5:30
11. John 4:32
12. Luke 17:21
13. John 8:58
14. Matthew 28:20
15. 1 Corinthians 12:12
16. John 8:12
17. John 14:6
18. John 10:30
19. John 5:30
20. John 14:10
21. Luke 17:21
22. John 17:15